ETHICS IN BUSINESS

ETHICS IN BUSINESS

Robert Bartels, *Editor*

Professor of Business Organization
The Ohio State University

BUREAU OF BUSINESS RESEARCH MONOGRAPH NUMBER 111

Published by
BUREAU OF BUSINESS RESEARCH
COLLEGE OF COMMERCE AND ADMINISTRATION
THE OHIO STATE UNIVERSITY
COLUMBUS, OHIO

COLLEGE OF COMMERCE AND ADMINISTRATION
JAMES R. McCoy, *Dean*

BUREAU OF BUSINESS RESEARCH STAFF
VIVA BOOTHE, *Director*
JAMES C. YOCUM, *Associate Director*

MIKHAIL V. CONDOIDE, *Economics*   RALPH M. STOGDILL, *Personnel*

PAUL G. CRAIG, *Economics*   MARTHA STRATTON, *Statistics*

J. L. HESKETT, *Management*   OMAR GOODE, *Tabulations*

MARTHA MOUNTS, *Assistant to the Director*
GRACE HULL, *Assistant to the Editor*
ESTHER EDGAR, *Librarian*

Research Assistants

RONALD BRADY   JAMES NEUHART
RONALD CARROLL   DAVID POTTER
JEANNE DAVIS   ALAN STEENSON
EDWIN J. GOTTFRIED   JAMES E. TROGUS

DEDICATED TO

VIVA B. BOOTHE

ON THE OCCASION OF HER RETIREMENT AS
DIRECTOR OF THE BUREAU OF BUSINESS RESEARCH

with the esteem and affection of her colleagues and associates, and in grateful recognition of her many contributions to the growth and development of the College of Commerce and Administration and The Ohio State University during 35 years of distinguished service as a member of the University faculty.

As Director of the Bureau of Business Research since 1936, Dr. Boothe perceived the problems of educational and research policy in a collegiate school of business with uncommon clarity and developed solutions that were optimal in the framework of the funds, personnel, and resources available. Under her direction the facilities and capabilities of the Bureau to conduct and implement quantitative research in the social and managerial sciences have been greatly expanded and improved. Dr. Boothe has given enthusiastic leadership and encouragement to the staff of the Bureau of Business Research. She has provided warm and timely counsel and assistance to the hundreds of students who were assistants in the Bureau over the years; and has been an inspiration to the faculty and graduate students of the College.

As Editor of Bureau publications since 1928, Dr. Boothe has maintained an unflagging insistence on the highest standards of excellence in writing and in form, and invariably made substantial contributions to manuscripts above and beyond the call of editorial duty.

As a member of the University faculty Dr. Boothe has contributed signally to the deliberations on many matters of important University policy. In her wide-ranging service on many University and faculty committees over the years, Dr. Boothe has had the wisdom and vision to see the truth and the courage to speak up for it; her counsel was always for the liberal and forward-looking, the excellent and genuine, the real and substantial, the forthright and direct, in University values and policies.

Dr. Boothe's academic career has been distinguished by a scrupulous integrity in all of her personal and professional associations, by an unqualified devotion to truth and responsibility. In civic affairs Dr. Boothe's service as District Governor, President-Elect and President of Altrusa International advanced the ethical-service ideals of Altrusa and was instrumental in building that organization to new heights of service and effectiveness. It is especially fitting, therefore, that a book on the subject of business ethics should bear this dedication to this distinguished woman, Viva B. Boothe.

May 1, 1963

FOREWORD

There are here preserved summaries of addresses presented for discussion in a graduate interdepartmental seminar on the general subject of Ethics in Business.

The variety of disciplines represented serves to emphasize the multi-faceted nature of the approach to the subject, involving, as it does, the genesis, content and formal expression of concepts of ethical behavior, the institutional framework by and through which they are formalized and transmitted, and the impact, once formulated, such concepts may or may not have upon individuals and upon our several social institutions—in this instance, the economic organization for business in a free society.

The very extensive annotated bibliography appended is, in itself, a substantial contribution to the serious student of the subject, regardless of the field of specialization.

VIVA BOOTHE, *Director*

March 15, 1963

PREFACE

This book is a representation of a graduate seminar devoted to consideration of ethics in business.

It is a unique publication in several respects. First, it is a fairly complete reproduction of the content of the lectures delivered to the seminar. Each of the addresses was prepared particularly for this purpose, and they are linked together by their relation to a unifying theme which ran throughout. Transcripts of the actual presentations, however, have been edited to enhance their readability. The discussions which followed each lecture were, for the most part, omitted in the interest of brevity, although cogent points debated were in some instances, through editing, incorporated into the body of the lecture itself.

A second unique aspect of the publication is the inclusion of a comprehensive annotated bibliography of books and periodical articles related to business ethics. The bibliography is a composite drawn from several sources. An initial bibliography compiled by the director of the seminar was supplemented by an extensive list of references assembled by Mr. Robert Pethia, a graduate assistant at The Ohio State University. This collection of titles was furnished to registrants in the seminar who, in turn, listed and annotated their own readings during the period of the seminar. A composite made from all these sources is presented in the Appendix.

The pattern of the seminar was designed. The logic and intent of the design are reflected in the nature and arrangement of the topics discussed. To begin with, the "problem" of business ethics was analyzed. That there is a "problem" seemed more than a presumption, in the face of current violations of common ethical standards in business and government. The "problem," however, is not explicit in any given situation; rather it is implicit therein. To state the "problem" of ethics in business today requires interpretation of the influences which give rise to the individual situations. The first lecture was devoted to consideration of this subject.

Granted justification for considering the question of ethics in business at all, a concept or definition of ethics was sought which would integrate subsequent discussions. As it developed, the definition of ethics did not lend itself to easy statement, and instead of one lecture being devoted to this, almost all speakers addressed themselves, in part, to the conception and definition of ethics, as they saw it. In the second lecture, a philosophic approach was taken and ethics was considered in the light of "the common good," as it is defined today.

Third, an historical analysis of business conduct in the United States during the last century, from the standpoint of ethical standards and behavior, revealed the way in which the "problem" has been regarded and coped with at various times. The thread of an increasing consciousness of social responsibility in business is apparent.

Following three introductory talks, three more lectures were devoted to the standards upon which business ethics may or must be based: the legal, the societal, and the theistic bases. Speaking of the first, a lawyer showed that even the law has a social background, but that the basic laws pertaining to ethics in American business require an ethics of *competition*. Two sociologists next discussed the ways in which societies evolve their standards of right and wrong in social action, giving particular attention to some of the ideological bases of our own social concepts. Finally, a religiously-oriented philosopher discussed the theistic basis of ethics which involves a concept of Deity and the various obligations which men assume by reason of their relation to God.

Following this, four areas of management decision involving ethics were analyzed—the relationships of management with customers, labor, competitors, and the community. Not only the problems but also the principles upon which judgment as to the rightness of certain actions were discussed.

The seminar was undertaken as a function of the Interdepartmental Seminar Committee of the College of Commerce and Administration, whose objective is to encourage curricular activity integrating the contributions of various social scientists, both within the College organization and those outside it. Thus have been brought to bear upon the subject of business ethics the viewpoints of philosophy, law, sociology and anthropology, religion, management, labor, finance, marketing, and community service. The co-operation of individuals representing these different viewpoints is appreciated, for their efforts made a success of this experimental interdisciplinary venture.

ROBERT BARTELS
Professor of Business Organization,
Director of Seminar on Business Ethics

February 1, 1963

TABLE OF CONTENTS

I

THE PROBLEM OF ETHICS IN BUSINESS

James W. Culliton

On many occasions when I have had discussions on ethics and business, I have felt that something was lacking. The discussion did not seem to get anyplace. The Danforth Foundation seminar held at Harvard Business School in 1957 was such a one. As one might expect at Harvard Business School, much time was spent on discussing specific cases. We examined religious and ethical as well as the business aspects of cases, without losing sight of the fact that some action had to be taken. This "what-are-you-going-to-do?" approach made men participants with responsibility rather than mere observers or outside experts. The experience was stimulating, interesting, and challenging.

I did not find it very helpful, however, beyond opening up some new questions through the exchange of opinions held by people with widely different backgrounds. Why? As I see it, we did not look at the fundamental framework in which we were trying to work, and it turned out that one man's opinion was as good as another. Few people are against morality or religion. So, by and large, we ended up in favor of honesty and the Golden Rule.

Last summer a Jesuit priest, who is studying for his doctorate at Harvard Business School, published an article based upon a statistical survey, trying to get an answer to the question "How Ethical Are Businessmen?" The survey brought out one problem: that it is almost impossible to survey businessmen's ethical practices without allowing one's own system of values to show in the interpretation of the results. Another problem was an overriding negativeness in many of the hypotheses or points of view.

Let me give you two illustrations. First, it is sometimes thought that being ethical puts limitations on what a competent businessman *as a businessman* ought to do. The Danforth Seminar brought out

1

the inseparability of decisions and reasons for them. One cannot first separately consider "What *business* decision do we want to make?" and then walk to the other side of the table and say "What *ethical decisions* do we want to make?" These two are inseparably bound together.

Another illustration of negativeness is the apparent opinion of many that business is either inheritantly bad or sets up circumstances which make a businessman find it more than ordinarily difficult to do what, *as a man*, he thinks is right to do. Also, as the priest's survey indicates, it is much more difficult to find out what men actually do believe than it is to find out what they say they believe.

Another illustration of my dissatisfaction grows out of a group called the Catholic Employers' and Managers' Association. This is a group of Catholic laymen who are trying to explore, largely on a case basis, how one would behave ethically *in specific business situations*. They have attempted a creed for American Catholic employers and managers. Why should there be a *Catholic* association? Are they, on the one hand, implying that they have a monopoly on ethics, or, on the other, are they displaying an inferiority complex, saying that they do not want to discuss this on the total open market place?

Finally, I would like to refer to Dr. Herbert Johnson's book on business ethics. He is on the Notre Dame faculty. This book tends to be, in my opinion, a little too dogmatic, a preaching with respect to a single ethical set of values. Now, as I have indicated, I have not found the discussion of *individual cases* very productive. This was true of Harvard; it is true of the Catholic Employers' Association. Nor have "sermons" been very helpful either, even though they do arouse some interest, especially if given by somebody like Henry Ford, who gave his business ethics speech in 1961.

The problem is how to take a positive rather than a negative approach to this subject.

One has to clear away superficialities and get down to fundamentals if he would (1) get a better definition of the problem, (2) establish areas of common agreement among various people interested in the problem, and (3) isolate and identify points of basic difference among such people.

If a person tries to discover what is right and what is wrong, what is better or worse in a specific situation, and tries to act accordingly, then he has already made a very basic commitment. If one is committed to try to do right and avoid evil, he has already made the most necessary commitment to ethics. He may make mistakes, he may be misinformed, he may seek goals which differ from yours and mine, but by this very commitment—that for ethical or moral reasons some things should be done and others should be avoided—he is taking a very big step.

I do not know whether each of you in this room has made that commitment or not. If you have not made such a commitment, my remarks will make sense only if they have a bearing on whether or not you want to make the commitment. If, on the other hand, you have made that commitment, you may well wish to review it in order to change it or reinforce it. My remarks will be couched in a language which more or less presumes a basic commitment to ethical conduct. Let us not lose sight of the fact, however, that such may not be the case, and, even if it is, the commitment need not be maintained. Let us see if we cannot get some of the fundamentals involved in the ethics of particular situations.

In any consideration of moral or ethical problems, there are two basic problems. The first has to do with the norms to be used; the second, with the application of norms to specific situations. Every human action is determined and judged by norms which lie outside the particular action itself. When I say *human action*, I mean to distinguish this from what is called the *action by humans*. Human action involves the intellect and will, whereas action by humans is the mere animal reflex, or natural, physical actions. You say you will or will not do something "because," and this "because" is always followed by some kind of theory or generalization which is outside the action itself.

Let me illustrate: "I will not walk under a ladder because it is unlucky"; or, "I will not walk under it to prove that I am not superstitious;" or, "I will not walk under it because there is a painter up there and he has paint. Because of the law of gravity, it might fall on me. I will not take that risk." Each one of these things following the "because" is a theory or generalization which we use to guide our particular actions. It is helpful to consider where these theories or generalizations come from, because they can be arrived at in several different ways. Some theories are based upon *superstition*. Some are *habit*: you just keep on doing what you did before without thinking very much about a particular decision. Some results from *social pressures*—you do what everybody expects you to do; some from *authority*—you do what you are told to do by somebody else. Finally, there is the *intellectual decision* as a basis for these beliefs—arrived at by investigating the evidence and deciding for yourself what your own generalizations are going to be. I may have stacked the cards a little as I have listed these, but among these the intellectual decision is the highest ranking of human values because here you are using the intellect and will, and this is the individual human being at work.

This leads to another important distinction. Especially in the field of business management, great emphasis is placed on decision making. But there are what are called *action decisions*, concerning what you are going to *do* in a particular situation. There is also another kind of decision which I call a *belief decision*: determining what theory or generalization will dominate your specific decision. Since action decisions rest upon the belief decision, the belief decisions are in many respects more fundamental. This brings us to one of the most basic problems in business ethics, namely, the difficulty of agreeing upon norms or belief decisions in a pleuralistic free society. This is illustrated in Exhibit A, "Norms by which Human Actions are Determined and Judged."

Exhibit A is a kind of map of the problem. It shows specific action decisions which are both determined by and judged by generalizations, theories, or norms which lie outside the particular situation. One of our problems is to get some kind of consensus as to what norms we are applying at any particular time. This indicates some of the problems involved. Actions based upon *more* (the first column) are contingent upon what people want at any particular time, and the norms are arrived at subjectively. They may change from society to society and from one time to another. The virtue of such norms may be economic success, or the fact of not getting caught doing what other people do not expect you to do at that

Exhibit A

NORMS BY WHICH HUMAN ACTIONS ARE DETERMINED AND JUDGED

HUMAN ACTIONS ARE DETERMINED } by NORMS outside themselves
and are JUDGED (good or bad)

SOME POSSIBLE NORMS

HUMAN ACTIONS
—as a man (include business actions)

	MORES	NATURAL LAW	DIVINE LAW
		Positive Civil Law	*Church Law*
Basis:	contingent	in accordance with nature (necessary)	in accordance with the supernatural (gifts)
How arrived at:	de facto	scientific investigation	revelation
Virtues:	variable (e.g. economic success, honor, not getting caught)	justice	love
Foundation:	consent (active or passive) (e.g. custom, habit, social pressures, superstition)	reason	faith
Standard:	subjective	objective	Divine will

J. W. Culliton

particular time. The foundation seems to be a kind of consent which may be actively sought for or just passively given. That standard tends to be subjective.

Another basis of action is the *natural law*, which is determined by scientific investigation of what you see in nature. Therein virtue is justice and its foundation is reason; the standard is objectively determined. Finally, there is the *divine law* which puts in the supernatural. You cannot ascertain this by scientific investigation but only by revelation. Its virtue is love and its foundation is faith.

One of the problems at the Harvard Seminar was that as soon as economists started to put love in some business analysis they got into trouble. This illustrates that in a pleuralistic society it is hard to get universal agreement concerning norms.

New let us take a look at the application of norms to specific situations. First I call your attention to a very fundamental truth: you cannot make valid moral judgments about something you do not understand. One of the real problems about ethics and morals in business is that the professional moralists, and what I call ethicians, do not understand business and management. Therefore they cannot give competent advice or make competent judgments. The reason for this is not hard to find.

Join me in the experiment of drawing a line down the middle of a piece of paper so that you can write words on both sides. On the left-hand side start with *individual independence, self-sufficiency.* On the other side, the opposite, of course, is *interdependence.* On the left side we have *small-scale operations*; the opposite of *large scale.* On the left we have the craftsman and a kind of *do-it-yourself* approach which goes along with self sufficiency; in contrast, we have the *specialist* and *management.* The left-hand side, relationships *face to face*; in management, the *organized structure of jobs* —you can think of organization without knowing who the organized people are. On the left-hand side, the *owner* or the *family* who are usually *identifiable*; on the right, the *corporation*—unidentifiable and artificial. On the left side, we have a *narrow range of facts*, which became available to most people, but by and large they were facts significant to what the recipients were interested in. On the other side, we are *deluged with facts*—our communication network is fantastic, but it reports a lot we do not know the significance of. Under the old scheme, work satisfaction was in *visable achievement*, and on the opposite side, *fractured contribution*, to a productive effort. On the left side, *static society*, and by and large a *static value system* that went with the static society. Now we have both *fluid society* and *value systems*. On the left side, we have the *stratified society*, in which there was little mobility for most people. We still have the stratifications but the people within them are *highly mobile*.

When scarcity was the keynote of our economic thinking, the *motivation* for work, frequently, was *fear*. I do not really know what kind of motivation we have in an affluent society. I think that this is one of the big problems which business and management have not faced up to yet, i.e., how do you get people to work when they are not afraid of losing their jobs? This scarce economy and the fear of losing the job put very real *limits on peoples' freedom* in the olden days; with our affluent society and the choices in the market place we probably have the *greatest amount of freedom—* real freedom—that any society has ever known. I am quite sure it frightens us a little. We have been talking about freedom for centuries, but now that we have had it we do not quite know what to do with it.

Factors listed on the left side have led to *individual decisions*; but now we are in *group decision-making* situations. The old type reasoning and examination tended to be rather *sequential*—one fact leading into another. Now we are beginning to recognize *simultaneous interrelationships* in an organic kind of sense. The virtues of the old were familiarity and stability; now we idealize it to new and obsolescence.

The column on the left contains those characteristics of a previous society about which you have heard many times. Those on the right give some of the characteristics of our industrialized society in which management is a new and different phenomenon. Management, as we now know it, did not even exist in society before.

It is to this complex, and not-too-well understood set of specific situations, that our not-too-well-agreed-upon norms have to be applied. That is what I think the problem of business ethics is.

There are people who look upon this picture and advocate going back to the good old days—the more stable society and the well-agreed-upon norms. I do not think that there is an alternative which we can safely advocate. Nobody has ever successfully gone back to any system once they have left it. This is even more unlikely when you look at some of the benefits our new system has produced, especially in the physical order of comforts, health, and opportunities. The solution is not to return to the horse and buggy era, in

Note: In the oral presentation of these remarks the audience was asked to write key words on the "right" and "left." For the convenience of the reader these are summarized below.

Characteristics of an Earlier Society	Characteristics of Industrialized Societies
individual independence self sufficiency	interdependence
small scale	large scale
craftsman	specialist
do-it-yourself	management
face to face relationships (people)	organized structure of *jobs*
the owner; the family (identifiable)	the corporation (unidentifiable-artificial)
narrow range of facts but significant	more facts, but less significant
work satisfaction in visible achievement	fractured contributions
static society (and values)	fluid society (and values)
stratified society, little mobility	stratified, but highly mobile
fear motivation in a scarce economy	? motivation in affluent society
real limits on freedom	the greatest real freedom known
individual decisions	group decisions
sequential	simultaneous inter-relationships
the old and stable	the new—obsolesence

order to be ethical, but rather it is to learn how to be ethical with automobiles, airplanes, and rockets.

The proposal to go back is not only impossible, it is defeatist. If you want to bring religion into this picture, there is even an insult to God involved in the idea of going back, because it would imply that God created some things—and man with an ability to understand them—but that they are basically unethical and immoral.

The challenge, as I see it, is that we have to be as dynamic, imaginative, and research-minded in the ethical field as we have been in the scientific and materialistic fields. We must accept this new world as a new opportunity for being ethical. The case is far from hopeless.

At the risk of sounding pontifical in closing, I wish to present five points for dealing with our very complex circumstances and problems.

1. You can get too logical and analytical about problems. If you take our achievements in business and science and asked someone to describe these to them in the abstract, the answer probably would be "It cannot be done." For instance, you might suggest building a business by putting liquid into bottles, bottles into cases, and carting them over the country, and when somebody takes the liquid out of them, you pick them up, bring them back, wash them, and do the whole thing over again. If you said you were going to do this for a nickel apiece, or even a dime apiece, people would say you are crazy. Yet Coca-Cola has built a pretty good business out of this practice. Or—describe our present telephone system, by which you can pick up the phone and be really disturbed if you do not get San Francisco or Hawaii in thirty seconds. This just is impossible if you take too logical a view of the total problem. By taking one thing at a time we have demonstrated that patient and hard meticulous work can accomplish much, even in complicated situations.

2. I am convinced that an awareness of the problem is a long step toward solving it. The mere fact that I was asked to come here, and that you had signed up for this kind of discussion, is, in itself a positive step toward getting some answers.

3. The moral and ethical aspects are not separable from business and management specifics. They are part of an interrelated whole.

4. There is no evidence of a basic conflict between business and ethics. We have to admit that we are real and imperfect people, so we are going to make mistakes, but even so there is not essential conflict. Business, as a way of life, can be the opportunity for behaving as the kind of man you would like to behave as. The real challenge, and at the same time the hope, lies in the concept of individual responsibility. And this is complicated by our trend to

ward group effort. But you cannot send a corporation to hell, or a committee to jail. We need new understanding of individual responsibility in group and interdependent relationships. One of the most vexing problems which I do not get very satisfactory answers about, is the question of how you allocate to individuals the moral responsibility for group decisions. This whole area of group decisions is one of the new factors in our modern life and needs to be researched.

This leads to another area of individual responsibility; competence in one's own job is an ethical responsibility. If you are going to be an ethical businessman you have to be first *a good businessman*. Medical ethics is concerned almost exclusively with how a good doctor would act in a specific situation. They have got away from the problem of having doctors who were completely incompetent. You do not discuss medical ethics in the area of whether a man is a competent doctor. Being a competent person in your job, I classify as one of the most important ethical responsibilities.

5. We all must face up to situations where we have to compromise what we would really like to do, if we are going to take any action at all. However, while compromise may be necessary *once,* there is another ethical responsibility—the necessity to work on the circumstances which made the compromise necessary in the first place. You must improve your *chances* of making better ethical decisions in specific situations in the future. The "everybody-is-doing-it" excuse not only leads to the continuation of bad ethics, but, more frequently than not, prevents businessmen from finding a much more successful *business* opportunity.

II

THE DEFINITION OF ETHICS IN BUSINESS

Anthony Nemetz

By way of defining ethics, I want to examine the nature of the common good in our day.

Let us assume that every society desires progress. Societies differ, however, in their concepts of what constitutes progress, just as individuals differ as to what constitutes happiness. Every one here is in favor of progress, but I seriously doubt that I could get any consensus on what you think are the ten most important social advances that have taken place in the twentieth century in the United States. How, then, do we as individuals tell what criteria are being implicitly or explicitly employed by our society as a whole to measure social progress? How do we get a perspective from which to see in what ways our society is developing the content of the common good?

There is no real need to get outside the society to see what is happening within. Reflection on the educational patterns and procedures within a society furnish us with a reasonably reliable index to those criteria. Consider, for a moment, the difference between the medieval society with its cathedral schools and our public school system. The content of educational process in the two cases is significantly different. Instruction in the cathedral school turned on the liberal arts, especially in the trivium (logic, grammar, rhetoric) which was to provide the student with the means of communication in his society. The mode of communication then was almost entirely verbal; the tone of the communication was juridical, whether ecclesiastical or civil. The means of persuasion were restricted to appeals to the received traditions. Instruction in the art of communication was juridical or legalistic, its purpose being to prepare men to facilitate the rule of Emperor, Prince, and Church, as well as to furnish men with pre-professional training.

Today, although we still hold to the notion that primary education is preparatory in character, the content of the arts has shifted in character. Communication is still the purpose, but the tone of the communication is anything but legalistic or juridical. As a result of the rise of the democratic system of government, together with the several industrial revolutions, the problem of communication has been directed to facilitating an exchange of views among the population generally, and to equip the broad share of people with the means of persuasion, analysis, and argument within a market place of goods and services.

Not only has the tone of education changed, but the instruments of education have also been transformed. In the medieval days, the instruments of education were set apart from the devices appropriate to commercial institutions. Now the radio, the television, and the press are simultaneously educational and commercial institutions. The media of popular communication are simultaneously educatiorltal and commercial.

The institutions of higher learning have been equally affected in recent years. Universities today are being organized in the pattern of the corporation image. By and large, who are trustees or regents of our universities if not corporation executives or corporation lawyers? Moreover, few college presidents are currently being appointed on the basis of their scholarly achievements.

I do not pass judgment on these developments, only note them. These facts are meant only to give reasons why the language of communication in argument, persuasion, and analysis in our day is basically economic, both at commonplace levels and at the sophisticated and planning levels. For example, how often do you or your professors say in response to an argument: "I just will not buy that."

My first point, then, is that the language we ordinarily use to express our day-by-day affairs is economic. There is an implied corollary in the fact. Every language, especially every language that was constructed for technical purposes, has basic terms, basic foci or modalities. Euclidean geometry, for example, uses as its basic terms the notions of point and line. So too, does the economic language we have inherited from the mercantilist and entrepreneural periods; it has as its basic terms the notion of productivity and allied concepts.

Before going on with the analysis, I want to suggest a principle about learning and thinking. I hold that in large measure thinking depends on hearing. I am not referring to the physical mechanism of the auditory sense, but rather to the meaning and reference of what is said. Meaning and reference depend upon linguistic habituation. Consequently, the language we use conditions, in part, the range of our thought, and again, in part, puts a limit on the forms of our reflection.

These two assumptions have some very provocative implications. The assertions that our basic language is economic and that we think according to the way we hear suggest two corollaries. The first is that the way in which we discover, define, and solve social problems is conditioned at least as much by our language as by the actual situation. Secondly, that in order accurately to refer to an existent situation and to grasp the significance of an evolutionary movement in society entails the need for a corresponding development in the basic terms used to describe and analyze the world about us.

The present use of an economic language with its basic notion of production is hopelessly anachronistic. To use outdated language, however, involves more than being old-fashioned. Inappropriate terms have a procrustean effect on stating and solving contemporary social problems. In short, our thinking about the current state of society is severly hampered by a lack in the devices of communication. Positively stated, the critical social problem in this decade is the redefinition of the relation between the public and the private spheres of activity or sectors of concern. In St. Thomas' terms, the common good needs redefining, and I do not believe we currently have any accurate way of even stating the problem.

One basic change in our society has largely contributed to the need for a redefinition of the common good. Our society can no longer be characterized as a goods producing society. In recent years, the majority of wage earners in the country are engaged in the rendering of service rather than in the production of consumer goods, and all the evidence suggests that in the coming decade the ratio of service jobs over goods producers may go to two to one. Increased technology is surely one of the reasons for this phenomenon, but the reasons for the change are less important than the consequences. The immediate consequences are easily seen. Techniques of advertising, devices in marketing, and attitudes in business management all have been profoundly affected. A shorthand way of saying all this is to talk about the affluent society as Kenneth Galbraith uses the term. For a society to be affluent requires that nearly all of its citizens have ready access to the necessities of life, and that a majority of the citizenry are in position to regard as necessities what were formerly the luxuries of a minority. Galbraith says that this situation has as a by-product the creation of a "dependence effect" by which he means that the need for new products or new styles or models must be developed before or alongside the production of the product itself.

The myth of an unsophisticated market has been completely debunked. A significant amount of goods now produced is no longer produced in a response to any native need. On the contrary, without an induced need many products would never be made. The role of advertising, too, has changed in our affluent, service-oriented society. There was a time when the function of advertising was simply to announce the availability of goods which were known and felt to be needed. A sale of cattle, of farm implements, of land, and even of Lydia Pinkham's remedy needed no especial explanation in the sod-busting days of "Gun Smoke." The needs were known, but the means of purchase were not always at hand, nor could the needed goods be readily supplied.

How different the situation today. Two years ago the steel industry produced all the needed steel for domestic and foreign consumption, while working only nine months at about 60 per cent capacity. Allow me to generalize on this example. A minority of our wage earners now can easily produce all of the needed consumer goods for the nation as a whole—and it is a minority that is proportionately decreasing. For the first time in history our nation can concern itself with more than the demands of life and can as a nation meaningfully direct its energies to realizing the good life.

It is precisely the affluence of the society which sets this challenge. And it is, furthermore, a consequence of the very possibility of nationally achieving the good life which demands a re-examination of what is properly public, and a definition of what falls within this sector of the common weal.

Probably the easiest way to get at this point is to see what historically was conceived to be the principal and proper functions of government. I would think that the national government would directly concern itself with the securing and maintaining of the common good. Looking to the philosophers in the British empirical tradition suggests that the common good was seen as the corporate view of private worth. Public concern and governmental action were directed to the defense and security of the private sectors. In other words, within the British empirical tradition, the common good was conceived as an extrapolation from the private good. I have the suspicion that the contractual theory of government in Locke and Hobbes is itself a kind of justification for this view. The fiction of the state of nature in which no one has ever been, but out of which everyone has had to come, is, I think, evidence of this position. Men, it was said, formed societies in order better to protect their own private interests.

And what were their interests? Life, liberty, and property. The tradition which links those three notions together has in some American quarters become as hallowed a revelation as that of Sinai. But are these three notions lumped together in any self-evident way? Is the notion of property derivable from the notion of life and liberty, or are these three aspects of some other more general notion?

Let me pass over these questions to the easier task of documenting my assertion that the notion of a common good was derived from that of a private good. Hobbes in speaking of the establishment of a "civitas" says that the business of the common power is "to defend (the citizens) from the invasion of foreigners, the injuries of one another, and thereby to secure them in such sort, that by their own industry and by the fruits of the earth they may nourish themselves and live contentedly" (*Leviathan*, page 118).

The reason for establishing a government, according to Hobbes, is a defective human nature. And the function of the formed government is simply to reduce the natural brutishness of man against man. Organized society is thus a multitude united by a common power. But a common power does not imply a common good which is essentially different from the aggregate of private goods. Quite to the contrary, Hobbes specifically says: "The nature of men being as it is, the setting forth of Publique land, or of any certain Revenue for the Commonwealth is in vaine; and tendeth to the dissolution of Government" (*Leviathan*, page 178).

Although Locke has a more generous estimate of humanity than does Hobbes, he too sees the common good as definable basically in terms of the private good. He insists that in society the source of value is private. He says: "Labor puts the difference of value on everything." Locke does hold that nature is bountiful enough to provide every man with his wants, if he labors. Yet despite these differences I think that Locke does not disagree with Hobbes' observation that man "whose joy consisteth in comparing himself with other men, can relish nothing but what is eminent" (*Leviathan*, page 117). Locke does make one most important qualification regarding the right of enjoying property gained through labor. He sets a limiting condition on what the individual has a right to keep. Using agriculture as his model, he says that a man can keep only what he can use, and if there is danger of spoilage, the surplus, which is the food that cannot be privately used, reverts to common possession.

Looking then to Locke and Hobbes, we can summarize their views of the common good by noting what they believed should be the concerns of government. It is the business of government to do for the multitude what no one individual can do for the corporate person, and that is to defend the corporate person from foreign attack. (Note that I am not saying that they said that it is the business of government to do for the individual what he cannot do for himself. That simply would not be true.) Secondly, the corporate body is entitled to share in the surplus of those private goods which were privately produced, but cannot be privately used and enjoyed because of the threat of spoilage.

One may ask whether these views did, in fact, influence the framers of our Constitution. There is good reason to suggest that our national thinking at the time of the framing of the Constitution looked to the private good for the model of public concern and common good. How else should we interpret the XXXV *Federalist* paper which deals with the question of who can most properly represent the people in the House of Representatives.

"The idea of an actual representation of all classes of the people, by persons of each class, is altogether visionary. Unless it were expressly provided in the Constitution, that each different occupation should send one or more members, the thing would never take place in practice. Mechanics and manufacturers will always be inclined with few exceptions, to give their votes to merchants, in preference to persons of their own professions or trades. Those discerning citizens are well aware that the mechanic and manufacturing arts furnish the materials of mercantile enterprise and industry. Many of them, indeed, are immediately connected with the operations of commerce. They know that the merchant is their natural patron and friend; and they are aware, that however great the confidence they may justly feel in their own good sense, their interests can be more effectually promoted by the merchant than by themselves. They are sensible that their habits in life have not been such as to give them those acquired endowments, without which, in a deliberative assembly, the greatest natural abilities are for the most part useless; and that the influence and weight, and superior acquirements of the merchants render them more equal to a contest with any spirit which might happen to infuse itself into the public councils, unfriendly to the manufacturing and trading interests. These considerations, and many others that might be mentioned, prove, and experience confirms it, that artisans and manufacturers will commonly be disposed to bestow their votes upon merchants and those whom they recommend. We must therefore consider merchants as the natural representatives of all these classes of the community.

With regard to the learned professions, little need be observed; they truly form no distinct interest in society, and according to their situation and talents will be indiscriminately the objects of the confidence and choice of each other, and of other parts of the community." (The Federalist, pp. 166-167.)

The point of the quotation does not need to be belabored. Presumably the business of the House of Representatives is to deal with the amalgam of concerns which makes up the common interests. But notice that the merchants are said to be the natural representatives of that common interest. In view of that fact, I do not think it extravagant to argue that the common good in our own nation was still modeled on the private good. For the function of merchants is to mediate the exchange of privately produced goods to private users for private ends and purposes.

To be sure we have changed our views over the past two centuries. The image of the merchant as the natural mediator between men and society is no longer an article of faith in the creed of conventional wisdom. It is now the lawyer who seems endowed by the oracle of popular will and aspiration. There is a certain amount of irony in this, for after the Revolution, many of the colonies having been surfeited on British justice outlawed the profession of barrister. It was a crime to be a lawyer; and now it is the lawyer who doth make criminals of us all!

We have changed in other ways too. On the surface, it seems obvious that legislative programs have been introduced which seem to have moved the nation away from the extremely limited notion of the common good that I have earlier cited. We have indeed added to the repertory of common concern. Programs of health, measures advancing universal education, and legislation providing for public recreational facilities have been enacted. This much is true. These measures have in effect extended the range of private exigency, but of themselves they do not contain a principle which establishes or vindicates a changed concept of the relation between the private and the public spheres of concern.

Horace Mann's appeal for universal elementary education was advanced on the hope that it would reduce crime and also that it would make the factory worker more productive. (Men who could read would not need as many foremen, and hence the labor costs would be cut.) More important examples may be taken from the New Deal of Roosevelt, under which the nation was introduced to an extended concept of the public good. Social security, unemployment compensation, antitrust legislation, graduated income taxes, and especially legislation regarding the right of eminent domain: all these on the surface suggest that the notion of the commonwealth has been extended well beyond the limits of defense and a sharing in the surplus of crops. I think it is true that some changes were made, but on reflection I regard them as marginal. The essence of the New Deal was simple enabling legislation. For a complex of reasons, the economic system had broken down and created flagrant inequities. Individuals, no matter how industrious and well-intentioned, could not satisfy their basic needs. The government, therefore, acted on behalf of such individuals and provided the sanctions under which individuals could more facilely acquire and hold the minima required for existence. I cannot overemphasize this last observation. The burden of New Deal legislation was not intended to give the individual a share in things held in common. Instead, it was to provide the limiting conditions, such as minimum wage, under which each individual could privately obtain privately produced goods for private purposes. The commonwealth was still seen as modeled on the private good. The legislation of the New Deal was much more corrective than it was distributive. There were evils which bedeviled the individual in his attempt to maintain life, and these needed correction.

These are two functions of the law, as seen by Cicero: the law discriminates between right and wrong; it distributes shares of the common wealth to the citizenry. In these terms, I am suggesting that the burden of our social legislation has been corrective. I suppose a case could be made that in some instances government was doing for individuals what they could not do for themselves, such as setting minimum wage laws. And, as a consequence, the government was at least enlarging the sphere of common concern, i.e., putting such matters on a par with national defense. But even if that point were raised, I would reply that the motivating arguments behind the legislation were not based on a concept of sharing in the common wealth, but were rather directed at facilitating the production and consumption of privately produced goods. The point of that legislation was precisely to stimulate the institutions of private production. The problem was to get the chickens off the farm and into the pot.

Now let us turn to the current situation. We live in a society whose basic mode of communication is economic. More than that, we discuss matters with a vocabulary in which the dominant modality is productivity. Our problem is that the old and familiar rhetoric is simply not adequate to the factual situation. What is the point of talking in terms of productivity when the fact is that there is a constantly diminishing possibility of productive opportunity? Here I must admit that I do not have all relevant figures under control. President Kennedy, in a recent press conference, suggested that we must create at least twenty-five thousand jobs a week simply to keep the current rate of unemployment from increasing. Whatever the accuracy of that figure, the basic problems of our society cannot be solved by an increase in the production of consumer goods. We are now and will continue to be a service-oriented society. The solution to problems such as unemployment due to automation cannot be solved by increased production of more consumer goods.

Today we are embarrassed by our own ingenuity. We can make more things with less human energy and effort than ever before. Some years ago I saw a cartoon in the *New Yorker* which exemplifies my view. The cartoon pictures a factory with an exit bin out of which washing machines were being ejected onto the street. The machines were piling up on the street in the fashion of ice cubes in the bag. And an embarrassed manager was sheepishly protesting that he forgot to turn off the switch on Friday evening. Indeed we can produce and do produce more than we need or want. The critical question is what shall we do with the people who cannot be employed in the production of consumer goods which no one needs or wants?

Allow me to make the moral in a slightly different way. In a goods-producing society, the value of services could readily be judged against produced goods. The economic value of a bartender in Dodge City could be measured by the cattle market, as could the worth of the stable man and even the Marshal. But today the situation has altered radically. By what can one judge the economic value of a service in a service-oriented society? As an example, take teaching. The social cry is unmistakable. We need more education to live in a technologically advanced society. Teachers are fond of protesting they are underpaid, and I must add justifiably so, but to what standard can we appeal? How can we reasonably say that we are not getting our just due? The man on the assembly line can count the finished pieces after a day's work. Yet students and understandably their parents would reject our counting noses and the rest of the corpses in a class as the criterion for wages. The kind of qualitative transformation which is demanded in teaching, and rightly so, is simply not susceptible to the quantification methods of time and motion study. The communication of ideals; the poetry of dreams; the distillation of commitments—these cannot be quantified by the measure of durable goods. No number of colored refrigerators are equivalent to a moment of a private dream turned into common vision, which is my view of the educational purpose.

My point, however, is not to pose as an academic Jeremiah. Of lamentations we have had enough! The problem is not vocational but national. It has two distinctive dimensions. In the first place, given both the acceleration of technological advance and the population increase, it can be confidently predicted that the actual number of jobs for the production of consumer goods will not rise proportionately to the population. Consequently, we are confronted with a seeming paradox. There will be an increasing availability of consumer goods while at the same time there will also be an increasing number of people without jobs. However, lest there be an economist in the crowd, or a travelling prophet for Parkinson's law, one qualification should be made.

This situation is parallel to the agrarian evolution of the last century. Farmers came to the city to work after the combine was invented. But where do the asphalt jungle cats go after the IBM machine has pre-empted their jobs? We now have an affluent society, one in which all needed consumer goods are readily available, and we also have an unemployment situation which is euphemistically described as chronic distress. It is difficult to see how any change in the tax structure or other alternating legislation could change the basic facts. For the first time in the history of any nation, this situation is unique. The available means of the production and distribution of consumer goods are adequate to the needs of the population and there is a surplus of available labor for more production—production which we simply cannot use.

The fact is that we have a surplus of manpower. We have a surplus of talent and of energy. The nation as a whole now has an untapped reservoir of talent which can no longer be fruitfully directed to the production of consumer goods. It is my contention that the argument Locke used about surplus farm products analogously applies in our situation to those talents and energies which are spoiling or about to spoil. Using Locke's principle we must at least come to terms with the fact of a surplus of unexpended and unusable effort and talent—talent, which by that principle, reverts to the commonwealth.

It is this fact which in itself demands a new approach to the question of the relation of the common good to that of private interest. I think it is possible to reject Locke's principle as the basis for the reconsideration, but I do not see how the basic situation would be altered by that rejection. The fact is that no matter what legislation is proposed, we as a nation simply can no longer argue that every man must be given an opportunity to be engaged in the production of goods. Symptomatic of this last observation is the history of labor itself. In the early years of this country, labor was conceived as being property. One need only mention the fact of indentured servants and slavery to document this assertion. Then came the labor movements and the concept of labor changed to that of an instrument of production. Incentive pay scales, piece work, time-and-motion studies—all were aspects of the concept of labor as a productive instrument. Today, however, labor is anxiously casting about for a redefinition of its own role in society. The question in automated factories is no longer how much can you produce. In fact, that question has only antiquarian interest. Given both the technology of our day and the added social demands on each citizen, the only real issue today is: "How hard ought a man to work?" But what criterion can be employed to answer such a question?

We read and hear much about featherbedding, not only in labor but in management as well. Within the organizations given to the production of goods, there is a fantastic amount of effort and energy which is not directly or indirectly used for the production of goods. I have the distinct impression that all parties are at least semi-consciously privy to the problem but hesitate to move because of no apparent solution. In addition to featherbedding there is also the problem of psychic satisfaction, or, more properly, dissatisfaction with the work at hand. What kind of personal involvement can be expected of a man whose task it is to drop an IBM card into the appropriate slot to initiate a programmed performance of production?

Lest I be grossly misunderstood, let me say at once, that I am not against progress, including automation. But let me equally insist that since we are now living in such a world, it simply does not make sense to invoke the rhetoric of an entrepreneural ear that has gone the way of the dinosaur. Let there be no mistaking the signs of our time. Our problem is no longer production, but one of distribution, and distribution of the wealth which is already common.

Up to now public policy has been based on an individual's right to engage in the productive arena and the exercise of that right. The Horatio Alger stories have served as the Liviticus of American enterprise. But we can no longer listen to Horace Greeley's injunction to go West, we are already there. There is no need to listen seriously to the nostalgic whimperings of the nineteenth century. We can still applaud the occasional self-made man as long as he is not too enamored of his maker. Less enigmatically put, I am insisting that the entrepreneural function can no longer characterize our society. Indeed, the entrpreneural concept itself has no compelling logic if all needed and wanted goods can be produced by a decreasing minority of the working force. There are, of course, still antediluvian bellows heard which say that we must maintain the historically proven standards of progress—private enterprise, indeed. But the voice of a mossbacked turtle is not always a kerygmatic trumpet.

What tentative conclusions can I draw from the analysis of our situation? The first is that as a nation we are almost embarrassed by our affluence of material goods. There are, to be sure, still numbers of those who have unfilled basic wants. Provision for these, however, can be made under existing legislation and institutional operations. My point rather is the direction the nation as a whole ought to take in defining the common good. And my argument is that the concept of private rights, especially private property rights, can no longer be the paradigm from which to build a concept of common good. On the contrary, the most urgent needs today seem rather to be a want of meaningful solitude; genuine education; a development of esthetic sensitivity, and especially the spiritual needs for friendship and love. Because of our technological advances and our scientific ingenuity we can as a nation not only turn our individual attention to the achievement of the good life, but indeed, must, as I see it, make the good life a matter of public concern.

The implication here is that we must construct a public philosophy in which the notion of the common good is prior to that of private right. For as citizens we are now able to share in wealth which far exceeds the notion of real property privately held. Remarks like these might in some minds conjure up visions of orbiting socialism. The fear of socialism in this context is not only anachronistic; it is foolish. What I am proposing is not that we take something away from those who rightly have it, but rather that we provide the means for sharing in what is already properly common. Nor do I want this understood as a rhetorical trick or as irresponsible casuistry. On the most ancient grounds, there has been a principle of distributive justice—a sharing of the common wealth. Now for the first time in history, we can make a significant move toward making the City of Man more nearly approximate the ideal of the City of God. And we can do this if we first create the rhetoric which will orient the national thinking away from the privacy of nineteenth century economic terms—the language of private production—and substitute for such terms the distinctions relevant to meaningful community.

The legislative task will be most demanding. We desperately need the definition of rights which entitle us to shares in what is alreadys ours, and we can have them if, and only if, the common good is redefined in our day.

To be a Thomist, and a follower of St. Thomas, means as I said at the beginning more than to be a metaphysician. It means striving to become a good man—it means trying to be proportioned to the common good. I cannot help but believe that if St. Thomas were with us these days, he would be deeply involved in the recreation of a public philosophy that would help to define the common good, so as to make the good life, a national life.

III

THE HISTORY OF ETHICS IN AMERICAN BUSINESS

Leo D. Stone

In our eager search for *truth*, whether it be applied to business or other areas of activity, it is sometimes helpful, and often reassuring, to see what can be learned from the lessons of history. If this is true in any field, it is certainly true in the areas of the study of American business ethics.

British Origins Of American Business Ethics

The beginnings of American concepts far antedate the arrival of the colonists on the New World shores. Settlers brought with them the traditions and mores of the British within the Anglo-Saxon framework. As early as 1340, for example, a *Manual for Confessors* defined "evils of trade" to include:

1. Selling as dear as one may or buying as cheaply as one may.
2. Lying or foreswearing to sell wares.
3. False weights and measures.
4. Selling on time.
5. Failure to comply with sample.
6. Hiding the truth about latent defects.
7. Making a thing look better than it is.

Price-fixing of foods was proper when done under proper authority, but forestalling, regrating, or engrossing were serious offenses. *Forestalling* started at the market or fairs. It was accomplished by physical obstruction of goods coming to the market, or by cornering or manipulating the market. Thus it deprived the owner of the market of his stallage, or rental for stalls. *Regrating* was the purchase of most or all of the goods at the fair or market for resale at a profit. *Engrossing* was obtaining control of the goods by contract

25

while they were still being grown or produced. The rules of at least one city provided the following punishments for forestalling:

First offense: Forfeiture of goods
Second offense: Punishment in the town pillory
Third offense: Fine and imprisonment
Fourth offense: Banishment

Because from 1200 to 1700 the laws against forestalling, regrating, and engrossing were fairly intact in England, they had their impact on the thinking of early American colonists. They were particularly applicable to the economy of acute scarcity in which the colonists found themselves. In 1631 the Virginia House of Burgesses ordered the English statute governing forestalling and engrossing into effect, and it was not repealed until 1644, after the supply of available goods increased.

Similarly, the American colonies were literally a result of the British monopolistic policy in colonization. The Virginia Company and the Massachusetts Bay Company came in the direct wake of successful operation under Royal Grants by the East India Company, the Levant Company, the Royal African Company, the Hudson Bay Company, and the Muscovy Company (Russian). In fact, the Hudson Bay Company did not lose its monopolistic privileges until 1869. Principals of the East India Company were prominent in the Virginia Company. The President of the Muscovy Company was Treasurer of the Virginia Company.

Although the colonists must have been strongly motivated for their own personal economic and spiritual advancement in most cases, they brought with them the prevailing philosophy of trade control as it was known in England. Prices and wages were frequently fixed by ordinance. Thus in 1634 the General Court of the Massachusetts Bay Colony fixed the price of beaver at 10s. per pound. By an order in 1630, master carpenters, masons, joiners, and bricklayers in the colonies were allowed 16 pence a day while ordinary mechanics and laborers were allowed 12 pence a day. In 1633, the rates were changed and other categories were added to the list. At the same time, the Court set a limit upon the percentage of profit that traders might claim on provisions, clothing, and tools. In 1692, Maryland passed "An Act Against Ingrossers and Regrators."

In Court in 1644, Robert Keane, "an ancient professor of the gospel, a man of eminent parts, wealthy and having but one child, and having come over for conscience's sake and for the advancement of the gospel," is charged with a heinous crime: he made over six-pence profit on the shilling, an outrageous gain. He was dismissed with a 200 pound fine, but not excommunicated. He became the subject of a sermon in which the false principles of trade were set forth:

1. To sell as dearly and buy as cheaply as one can.
2. If a man lose some of his commodities by casualty at sea, to raise the price on the rest.
3. To sell as he bought, even though he paid too dearly.

To seek riches for riches' sake was the sin of avarice.

Similarly earmarked with their British origin were the early colonial regulations regarding weights and measures, quality standards of such commodities as bread and beer, and laws prohibiting adulteration and deceit. Production was frequently stimulated by bounties, premiums, and subsidies. A Maryland statute of 1671 provided a bounty of one pound of tobacco for each pound of hemp produced in the province and two pounds of tobacco for every pound of flax. Virginia in 1662 offered five pounds of tobacco for every yard of woolen cloth woven by its inhabitants. Most bounty laws related to textiles and reflected the desire of the colonists to become independent of English cloth. The standards of manufacture were elevated by premiums for products of exceptional workmanship. Public lands were frequently granted in aid of manufacturing projects. The privilege of extracting ore from common lands was occasionally conferred for similar reasons. It was not uncommon for a colony or its towns to make a public loan for a new industry requiring a large amount of capital. A more novel form of paternalistic aid to industry was the practice of making various commodities, such as flax and hemp, legal tender for the payment of taxes and debts. The manufacture of such products was even exempted from all taxation.

The Tudor monopolies had their counterparts in colonial history. The exclusive privilege of manufacture and sale was granted:

1. Salt—Massachusetts, Connecticut, Virginia, South Carolina
2. Castile soap—Rhode Island
3. Sawmill, grain mill, tobacco pipe factory—South Carolina
4. Tar, pitch, rosin, turpentine—Massachusetts
5. Linseed oil mills—New York
6. Potash works—Connecticut

The development of the colonial industry was impeded by adverse restrictive legislation of the mother country. Parliament was induced by English tradesmen to enact laws preventing the manufacture of products competing with English goods. In 1699, exportation of wool, yarn, or cloth produced in the colonies was forbidden. Exportation of hats was forbidden in 1732. Colonists were permitted to ship pig and bar iron, but they could not erect rolling mills and steel furnaces. This prevented the colonists from making their own tools and implements and also kept England supplied with iron.

Industrialism did not develop in the colonies until after the Revolution. Toward the end of the 1700's, the factory system became firmly established in the textile industry; then it spread rapidly throughout the industrial orders. By 1840, the home, except in the frontier communities, had been replaced by the factory system. Machinery had superseded handicraft production.

The Age of Certitude

In the early years of the American economy, the people were living in a relative "Age of Certitude." Economic life was on a narrow and restricted basis. As the beginnings of a more extensive commerce appeared, the ethical standards were dictated by the Church. R. H. Tawney expressed the situation in his *Religion and the Rise of Capitalism:*

> "Hence all activities fall within a single system, because all, though with different degrees of immediateness, are related to a single end, and derive their significance from it. The church in its wider sense is the Christian Commonwealth, within which that end is to be realized; in its narrower sense it is the hierarchy divinely commissioned for its interpretation; in both it embraces the whole life, and its authority is final.

Though practice is a variance with theory, there is no absolute division between the inner and personal life, which is 'the sphere of religion', and the practical interests, the external order, the impersonal mechanism, to which, if some modern teachers may be trusted, religion is irrelevant."

From the time of the Middle Ages, when usury was a sin and when buying and selling as a merchant stamped a man as a candidate to be cast out of God's temple, to the time of the colonists, a complete reversal of attitude took place. Acquisition, increase of money, mercantile achievement—these became major virtues.

Cotton Mather was a high priest of the colonial American of the 1700's. He expressed the view that wealth was a sign of divine favor and getting it was a way of glorifying God. He declared: "Sirs, you cannot but acknowledge that it is the Sovereign God who has bestowed upon you the riches which distinguish you." Another time, he said: "I tell you with *diligence* a man may do marvelous things. Young man, work hard, while you are *young*. Let your business engross most of your time." He thought that the accumulation of wealth should be determined by "Exact rule." Men must resolve "that they will never be richer than just so far." They must devote the excess to "pious uses" of paying, lending, giving, and forgiving. But if anyone should fail to provide for his own and his posterity, he has denied the faith. Charity began at home!

"Don't misapply your charity. For the poor that can work and won't, the best liberality is to *make* them. A method must be found whereby idle persons may obtain their bread, but it is up to the authorities to find the method. As for idlers, common beggars, and the like, here we must follow God's command. Let them starve."

The attitude of that day toward human rights was well expressed by a prominent merchant, John Saffin. He said: "To declare that all men have equal rights to liberty and all outward comforts of life goes against divine wisdom, for God has ordained different degrees, some to be high and honorable, some to be low and despicable; some to be monarchs, Kings, Princes, Governors, Masters, and Commanders, and others to be subjects to be commanded, servants of sundry sorts and degrees bound to obey; yea to be slaves; otherwise there would be mere parity." Every member of the body is useful, but this does not mean that all are of equal and like dignity.

Another vein of thought was developing about the same time which did not carry with it the harsh implications of Mather's position. John Wesley had expressed what seemed to him to be a curious dilemma:

1. Religion makes a man frugal.
2. Frugality begets wealth.
3. Wealth makes a man indifferent to religion.
4. Religion destroys itself.

The life of John Woolman of New Jersey, a contemporary of Wesley, showed the reaction to this tendency. He had a mercantile store, his tailoring business, and a law practice. Believing one of William Penn's precepts, he adopted it in practice. The precept is: "Merchants are tenants of the public." He wrote in his journal:

> "Having got a considerable shop of goods, my trade increased every year and the road to large business appeared open, but I felt a stop in my mind . . . The increase in business became my burden; for though my natural inclination was toward merchandise, yet I believed truth required me to live more free from outward cumbers . . . In a while I wholly laid down merchandise . . . I found it good for me to advise poor people to take such things as were most useful, and not costly."

During the eighteenth and into the latter half of the nineteenth century, the two traditions, as expressed by Mather and Woolman, and many others, maintained a healthy tension motivating them to *good* deeds. A feeling of the essential holiness of wealth-gathering and a sense of stewardship toward those less fortunate in the economic race and on lower rungs of the social ladder characterized their concern. Jonas Chickering, the piano maker, one time wrote his debtors: "If you cannot pay me now, pay me when you can. If you are never able to pay me, I shall not trouble you."

An early privateer, Joseph Peabody of Salem, was lauded for his charities and his refusal to take to litigation.

Alexander Brown of Baltimore, in the Irish-lace import business, won warm respect in 1834 when he pledged his personal credit to make good the obligations of the failing Bank of Maryland.

Thomas Eddy, in New York, lost one fortune as an exporter and made another as an insurance underwriter. He was honored for "ameliorating the moral and physical condition of New York, backing the Erie Canal, improving the penitentiary system, as well as being a model of commercial integrity."

The Brown brothers of Providence, wealthy shippers and importers, especially prospered in whale oil. They founded Brown University and subsidized the early spinning industry.

Amos Lawrence of Boston—a leading wholesale merchant—was deeply worried about his faithfulness in the *proper use of his wealth.*

Directly in line with the tradition of Cotton Mather and of Calvinism were the attitudes of Benjamin Franklin. He looked upon his business as the foundation of all else that he did. In his last will and testament, he started: "I, Benjamin Franklin, printer . . ." He wrote:

"My original habits of frugality continued and my father amoung his instructions to me as a boy, frequently repeated a proverb of Solomon, 'Seest thou a man diligent in his calling, he shall stand before kings, he shall not stand before mean men.'"

"Industry and frugality are the means of producing wealth and thereby securing virtue."

Franklin also tells of running his competitor in printing work out of business, a man named "Keimer." "I desire with all humility," he said, "to acknowledge that I owe the mentioned happiness of my past life to His kind providence, which leads me to the means I used and gave them success." Thus it is apparent that in Franklin's mind there was no conflict between wealth and the spirit of his religious world.

Divine Right of Businessmen

Alongside these moral traditions a new philosophy also burgeoned. It came with the factory system. It might be called the "divine right of businessmen." George Baer expressed the philosophy thus:

"The rights and interests of the laboring man will be protected and cared for—not by the labor agitators, but by the Christian men to whom God in his infinite wisdom has given the control of the property interests of the country."

A far greater number, however, traced their trusteeship to God very *indirectly,* finding instead a sanction for their activities in social

Darwinism (the survival of the fittest) supported by the doctrines of Adam Smith and the "laissez-faire" economists.

Daniel Drew and John D. Rockefeller may be cited as examples of highly religious men of the nineteenth century who lived and died fully believing in the divine right of businessmen.

It has been suggested on numerous occasions that the early positions of Calvinism and the well-accepted religious doctrine favorable to individual initiative, habits of industry and thrift, virtually endless accumulation of wealth, and even (in some cases) condemnation of the poor led to an early emancipation of economic life from church control. There was the comforting assumption of a pre-established harmony between the efforts of individuals to seek their own advantage and the welfare of the community as a whole. Economic injustices were assumed to be automatically eliminated if economic laws were allowed to run their courses unhampered. Thus the economic order came to be regarded as having laws which were autonomous in relation to any detailed guidance or criticism from the Church, and the free working of the economic system was considered to be an excellent example of the existence of a divine Providence. This was a natural development, because there was no way of recognizing divine judgment upon the economy except in terms of the laws of economic order. With the onrush of the development of capitalistic institutions, the Church became even less inclined to be critical, partly because of difficulty in keeping abreast of what was happening in business institutions and practices.

With the development of this new complacency toward religious obligation, the obligations of stewardship to fellow members of society became more formalized—more of a Sunday religion, and less to be a counterweight in the everyday conduct of affairs—with a resultant inconsistency between weekday practices and Sunday beneficences. With the emergence of the factory system, the concept of obligations to members of the family who worked in the home as an economic unit did not survive the transferance to a new productive process. The workmen in the plant did not assume their appropriate place as logical beneficiaries of the managerial stewardship, as in the family system, although in other respects their obligations as servants remained. Aside from the chattel slavery condition in the

South, there was also the development in the mid-1800's in England and America of the "fellow servant" rule, where an employee had the gall to sue his employer for negligence of a "fellow servant." Out of this situation the courts found basis for suit against the employer only after the master had interposed three distinct defenses:

1. The rule of assumption of risk—The master is not required to answer to an ordinary risk which the servant may be said to have assumed upon accepting the contract of employment.
2. The fellow servant rule—The master cannot be held to the negligence of a fellow servant of the injured party.
3. Contributory negligence.

It is easy to see how, with the law setting up such rigorous tests for liability, workmen's compensation acts later became a necessity.

The underlying economic doctrines which supported the concept that natural law worked to the mutual good stemmed from Adam Smith's great treatise, *An Inquiry into the Wealth of Nations*. This work took five years in the writing. It was originally published in 1776, in America in 1789, but its overwhelming influence in American thinking came with the development of the factory system many years later. The precepts which lent themselves so well to advocates of big business were basically these:

1. Improvement in the productivity of labor depends largely on the division of labor.
2. Before the efficient division of labor can be carried out capital must be accumulated. There must be an accumulation of stock.
3. The productive factors (land-labor-capital-enterprise) flow to the area of highest productivity.
4. This flow and the pricing of goods is accomplished through the natural equating of supply and demand factors as if guided by an "unseen hand."
5. The function of the state generally is to permit the forces to operate by:
   a. Guaranteeing property rights
   b. Enforcing contracts
   c. Providing police protection

Thus, by the mid-1800's or earlier, a combination of circumstances provided the basis for the lapse in business morals of the last of the 19th and the early part of the 20th centuries. The following developments occurred:

1. Church complacency.
2. Growth of the factory system and substitution of impersonal (institutional) relationships in place of personal ones.
3. The legal lag.
4. Economic theory which saw a full stream of economic goods flowing in a naturally equilibrated society.

These conditions provided a natural opening for moral and ummoral men alike.

Fortune magazine has commented: "By the end of the nineteenth century God was no longer in business in any real sense . . . " Such judgment need not be limited to the "robber barons" who could hardly be said to be practicing a form of capitalism in any real sense, but who mostly were engaged in a juvenile warfare, "like small boys joyous in chicanery." Even so conscientious a man as Thomas Mellon of Pittsburgh, who lived assiduously by the maxims of Ben Franklin still found it difficult to keep his proportions straight in the post-Civil War period. Owning a large slice of Pittsburgh real estate, he insisted that properties be foreclosed on mortgagors only if they were "weakened by bad habits and extravagant living." But there were a great many weak men in Mellon's eyes. These were the characteristics of the Golden Age of American business:

1. Lost certainty of purpose.
2. Gained power, and learned that power corrupts.
3. Confused means with ends; sought wealth beyond needs of bodily comfort.
4. Built resentments leading to legislation, muckraking, and later New Deal.

The "Robber Barons"

Daniel Drew was famous for his *watered* stock. Later on in his life he gave his note for $250,000 to the seminary that bears his name. He never paid the note but died bankrupt.

This was a period of maneuvers, not rationality. Neither Vanderbilt nor Drew kept any books at all. Charles Francis Adams, writing in 1915 of this earlier period, had this to say:

> "I am more than a little puzzled to account for the instances I have seen of business success—money-getting. It comes from a rather low instinct. Certainly, so far as my observation goes, it is scarcely met within combination with the finer or more interesting traits of character. I have

known, and known to tolerably well, a great many 'successful' men— 'big' financially—men famous during the last half century, and a less interesting crowd I do not care to encounter. Not one that I have ever known would I care to meet again either in this world or the next; nor is one associated in my mind with the idea of humor, thought, or refinement. A set of money-getters and traders,—they were essentially unattractive."

This is perhaps a too sweeping indictment of the period. There is little doubt, however, that the period marked the low point in American business morality.

Daniel Drew said, "Sentiment is all right up in the part of the city where your home is. But downtown, NO. Down there the dog that snaps the quickest gets the bone. Friendship is very nice for a Sunday afternoon when you're sitting around the dinner table with your relations, talking about the sermon that morning. But nine o'clock Monday morning, notions should be brushed aside like cobwebs from a machine. I never took any stock in a man who mixed up business with anything else. He can go into other things outside of business hours. But when he's in the office, he ought not to have a relation in the world—and least of all a poor relation."

A few retained the older sense of morality and applied it to business. In 1860, Richard T. Crane, a manufacturer of plumbing supplies, made *good* products. He ran an honest factory, left his employees a pension fund, and generally treated himself as one of the workmen.

Perhaps with the Cullom Committee in 1887, whose investigation of the Standard Oil Company and the railroad rebating practices of the time, the federal government signalized its first official moral concern and determination to become active in the public interest. The Interstate Commerce Commission was established and the Sherman Antitrust Act was passed.

The early establishment of the ICC undoubtedly stems from the fact that the early "robber barons" were railroad men.

The "Four Hundred" was started in 1876 at a Centennial ball. Often the captains of industry were not admitted, but their sons were. Jay Gould was too unscrupulous, but his son George was admitted. Colonel Cornelius Vanderbilt was too profane and scornful, but his son William belonged. The Astors and the Vanderbilts accepted each other at the same functions by 1883.

Of the attitudes and interests of these men, Theodore Roosevelt said:

> "I am simply unable to make myself take the attitude of respect toward the very wealthy men which such an enormous multitude of people evidently really feel. I am delighted to show any courtesy to Pierpont Morgan or Andrew Carnegie or James J. Hill, but as for regarding any one of them as, for instance, I regard Professor Bury, or Peary, the Arctic explorer, or Rhodes, the historian—why, I could not force myself to do it even if I wanted to, which I don't."

Price tags became important to those at the top and were respected by the bulk of the rest of society, still secretly longing and expecting ultimately in some way to share in this wealth by the great equilibrating process. Terms of great significance were: Mr. Gould's $500,000 yacht; Mr. Morgan's $100,000 palace car; Mr. Vanderbilt's $2,000,000 home, $50,000 paintings.

Social power fell on the American businessman right at the time he was least certain of what his duties might be.

The Reform Period

Out of the rampant activities of the late 1800's came many reforms. Of course, the Sherman Antitrust Act of 1890 provided a legal landmark. But a new interpreter from the standpoint of the economists and the man who later was to have a great impact on complacency in regard to the workings of natural economic law was Thorstein Veblen. Instead of visualizing, as Adam Smith did, that the capitalist is the generator of economic progress, Veblen found the businessman no longer playing the role, but instead acting as a saboteur of the system. Veblen saw the economic process as basically mechanical in character—a huge machine turning out goods. Businessmen were concerned with making money, whereas the machines and their engineer masters were only involved in the end process of making goods. The "robber barons" were not interested in the productive processes.

At the time Gould was fighting Vanderbilt for control of the Erie he received this letter from his superintendent:

"The iron rails have broken and laminated and worn out beyond all precedent until there is scarcely a mile of your road, between Jersey City and Salamonca or Buffalo, where it is safe to run a train at the ordinary passenger or train speed, and many portions of the road can only be traversed safely by reducing speed of all trains to 10 to 15 miles per hour."

At the very time Henry Villard was heralded as an organizing genius for completion of a a transcontinental line for the Northern Pacific, James Hill, a rival railroadman, said: ". . . the lines are located in good country, some of it rich and producing good tonnage; but the capitalization is far ahead of what it should be for what there is to show and the selection of grades and routes is abominable. *Practically it would have to be built over.*"

A sterling example of Veblen's point was the formation of the U.S. Steel Corporation in 1901. Against real assets of $682 millions were sold bonds of $303 millions, preferred stock of $510 millions, and common of $508 millions. The financial company was over *twice* as large as the operational company. J. P. Morgan's underwriting profit was $62,500,000. Even this might have been condoned by Veblen if it was efficiently run after it was organized, and the benefits had been passed on to the customers of the company. This did not happen. For 13 years after the formation of the company, the price of steel rails remained $28 per ton, even though it cost less than half that much to make them. In other words, the operational advantage was subverted in effect to maintain an artificial financial structure. Another prime example of the same effect is found in the history of James Duke and the formation of the American Tobacco Company.

The tone of the redefinition of ethical standards at the end of the 19th century, as required by the excesses of the tycoons of the day, was defined by court interpretations of the Sherman Act.

The Addyston Pipe case determined that the pipe pool was illegal under the Sherman Act. The case was decided in 1899. From the earliest times, conspiracies preventing the free and unhampered movement of price have been illegal. Prices fixed by law have the status of "just prices," otherwise they should be competitively determined.

The Northern Securities case in 1904 settled the issue that the corporate form of handling did not provide a dodge for monopoly or combination in restraint of trade. Labor was held to be covered by the Act.

In 1911, the United States Supreme Court broke up the tobacco and oil empires by announcing the "Rule of Reason." Factors considered under the rule of reason were:

1. Intent to monopolize.
2. Lessening to existing competition.
3. Extent of market control.
4. Abuse of power.

Items 1 and 4 seemed to be dominant in the result. This was distinctly an era of *good* and *bad* giants. The U.S. Steel Company in the early 1920's was found to be a *good* giant, in spite of the earlier Gary dinners and a 50 per cent control of the market.

In 1914, the Clayton Act was passed to meet specific needs:

1. Need for economic interpretations.
2. Not only large, but smaller corporations were engaging in unfair practices.
3. Injunction process was brought to bear on practices not unfair at common law: a. Bogus independents, b. preferential rates, c. local price cutting, d. fighting brands, e. exclusive dealing arrangements, f. tying contracts, g. price discrimination, h. inducement of breach of contract, i. intimidation.
4. Labor unions were taken out of the prescribed category for combination—but the injunctive process to prevent "irreparable damage" to property was freely used until the Norris-La Guardia Act of 1932.

Gospel of Production

In the early 1900's, Henry Ford, a leading advocate of the gospel of production, said: "The best way to make money is not to think much about it. Organize to do as much good as we can for everybody." His philosophy of manufacture included: 1) quantity production; 2) few parts per car; 3) progressive methods; 4) common sense sales methods; 5) ample sales outlets; 6) smaller profit per unit; 7) cash discount on all bills; 8) no loans; no interest; 9) no extravagance. Ford felt his position obligated him to take public stands on moral issues:

1. Employees could not spend their evenings "unwisely."
2. No money was to be spent on the "old country."
3. Money should not be spent foolishly.

4. No drinking, neither on the job nor at home.
5. He sent a peace ship to Europe to settle World War I.
6. He tried to popularize square dancing to wean people away from jazz.
7. He was opposed to "international financiers."
8. Collector and food faddist.

Contrary opinions of Ford's decisions at the time they were made include:

1. The decision in the Dodge Brothers vs. Ford Motor Company case. In this case the court held: "It is not within the lawful powers of a corporation to shape and conduct a company's affairs for the merely incidental benefit of shareholders and for the primary purpose of benefiting others."
2. John M. Edgerton, then president of the National Association of Manufacturers said: "Ford may try to amend the Decalogue, but any general acceptance of a five-day week means surrender to easy and loose living."

The gospel of production did much during its period to weight the scales in favor of the efficient, well-run, large corporation. It does not always explain appropriately the controls that are essential to the capitalistic system:

1. Allocation of resources—free entry and exit.
2. Plant efficiency—the most economical size—are there always combination economies?
3. The influence of product differentiation and the problems created thereby.

The Gospel of Distribution

Many of the problems arising from the failure of the controls become apparent in the collapse of 1929 and in the years leading up to the New Deal. This became the period in which much was said about "poverty in the midst of plenty." During this period and the years of emergence from the depression, businessmen underwent a re-examination of their goals.

Filene of Boston said: "Business is a public trust." H. S. Dennison of Dennison Manufacturing Company said: "The problem of ownership and control of property are, for the Christian teacher and social engineer alike, problems of organizing the forces and influences which work upon men so that they will lead toward a progressively greater utilization of the powers of each individual for the deepest good of all."

Thereupon, Dennison redistributed stock among his working executives, set purchasing, sales, and credit policies, so as to offset seasonal and cyclical employment, and to develop a cooperative atmosphere.

Jay Hormel, in 1937, declared, "The idea that the employer is lord and master of his own business is an antiquated notion." In a seasonal industry (meat packing) he introduced a guaranteed annual wage. He took the lead in canned meats to set up a productive process to reduce seasonality in his services.

Roosevelt—Keynes on Unemployment and Investment

Almost simultaneously, in point of history, Franklin Delano Roosevelt was applying a remedy and John Maynard Keynes was giving a new diagnosis to the economic maladies of the United States. In his *General Theory of Employment, Interest, and Money,* Keynes said, "There is no flood of savings seeking investment at the bottom of an economic trough." The old theory in that regard does not work. The economy has reached maturity. There is an inadequacy of new projects for investment. Roosevelt had deliberately embarked the government on an expansive program of "priming the pump."

Rexford Tugwell, a Rooseveltian advisor, in an address entitled "Discourse on Depression" (April, 1932) called for:

1. Strenuous opposition to the reduction of wage levels.
2. Strenuous measures to force down retail prices until the index of their fall equalled that for wholesale prices.
3. Organized federal relief; a vast program of public works, coupled with relief on a family basis.
4. Securing funds by drastic income and inheritance taxes.
5. Avoidance of budgetary deficits and monetary inflation.
6. Taking over by government of any necessary enterprises which refuse to function when their profits are absorbed by taxation.

This summary of recommendations typifies the culmination of institutional economic thought, disagreed with for so long a period by the traditionalist. It perhaps can best be summarized as:

1. The philosophy of pragmatism.
2. The psychology of behaviorism.
3. The economics of institutionalism.

A whole new conception of "business rights," "property rights," and the "role of government" entered now. Government received an unexpected rebuff. Scared by the new program, business was reluctant to undertake new private investment. The atmosphere in Washington was "anti-business." Cooperation with labor unions was implored. New rules and regulations were emitting daily. Higher taxes were inevitable.

The story of the 1930's seems to be that the Government did a partial investment job in the hope that business would do the rest. Business, on the other hand, was shaking in its shoes, with the result that a full recovery was not realized short of World War II.

It was during this time that new ethical concepts in regard to the new "cooperation" with labor were codified in the Norris-La Guardia Act, and new concepts of unfair pricing practices were recognized in the Robinson-Patman Act, and the state fair trade laws. The NRA was to regulate codes of business providing for, among other things, price fixing and market allocation.

The Norris-La Guardia Act abated the use of the injunctive process in labor disputes as to employees with direct or indirect interests in the outcome. In the Apex Hosiery Company case, the U.S. Supreme Court declined to uphold a trebled judgment for $711,932 against a labor union caused by a 1½ month "sitdown" strike. The union had only 8 of 2,500 employees; 80 per cent of hosiery was in inter-state commerce. Yet the court held that there was no violation of the Sherman Act. The restraint was not such as was proscribed by the antitrust law. They were not policing inter-state commerce under this statute.

The Robinson-Patman Act and NRA were both expressions of the goal of government to strengthen the weak competitor at the expense of the strong. Thus, in this time of economic sickness, it becomes apparent that new medicine must be administered to preserve the competing elements of the system. With the declaration of the NRA as an unconstitutional act and the later supersession of the Norris-La Guardia Act by the Taft-Hartley Act, it became apparent that, in some cases at least, the remedy was more deadly than the disease.

Out of these economic, legal, and cultural developments has come the new doctrine of the responsibility of management to the many contributors to its reason for being. A writer in *Fortune* mag-

azine called it the "Gospel of Service." The service is no longer only
to the shareholders and perhaps incidentally to others who will
benefit indirectly through receipt of the company profits. The service is now to: 1) consumers, 2) employees, 3) the community, 4)
the nation, and 5) shareholders. Owen Young of General Electric
said:

> "Managers are no longer attorneys for stockholders. They are trustees
> for a great institution."

Young saw three classes of beneficiaries: 1) investors, 2) employees, and 3) consumers. He saw the purposes of management to be
to keep these interests "in balance." Admitting that such conduct is
designed to win public favor, he considered gaining favor for such
an achievement morally defensible.

Lou Shannon of DuPont recently cited a case in which the company placed a new plant in the least desirable of three locations to
provide continuing employment to a substantial work force which
had a long record with the DuPont Company. Charitable foundations, educational grants, messages to the public of an informative
nature on social subjects exemplify this attitude.

Our historical review does not dare approach too near the present lest we lose our status as student of the *historical* evolution. We
must therefore leave the businessman at this juncture, struggling
with his balance of the claims of each member of society to whom
he owes a responsibility.

IV

THE LEGAL BASIS OF ETHICS

Carl D. Fulda

It is perhaps not quite accurate to speak of the "legal basis of ethics," for the law is not a self-contained unit but rather mirrors the ideas of the entire society. To this extent it is questionable and unsound to distinguish the law from other social sciences in considering the bases of ethics. In other words, the law reflects the thought prevalent in the community, including its moral values, and thus it becomes a basis of business ethics.

In approaching this subject of the legal basis upon which some of the ethical decisions in business are based, let us consider first the basic law of business regulation. This law is what I sometimes call the Eleventh Commandment: Thou shalt behave like a competitor—thou shalt compete. To state negatively: Thou shalt not behave in a manner incompatible with the idea of free competition.

To appreciate how we have arrived at such a public policy, let us consider some of the events of the past hundred years. The development of this country subsequent to the Civil War was characterized by the continuation of the Industrial Revolution, the expansion of the railroads, and the transition for the first time from a predominantly agricultural and handicraft society to one of very large corporations. This extraordinary development had its counterpart in a variety of abuses which followed in the wake of this development. People began to fear the large concentrations of economic power, particularly of the railroads which at that time occupied a monopoly position. There were yet no trucks, airplanes, or private automobiles. To some extent there was water competition, but that was not very significant. The railroads had a monopoly of transportation, and while they rendered enormous service to the country they also abused in those early days that position by all sorts of practices which may be summarized briefly as follows:

43

They charged excessive rates, because there were few if any users of their service who had sufficient bargaining power to bring their rates down to reasonable levels.

They engaged in discriminatory treatment by charging lower rates to those enterprises with which they were allied. There was a very considerable connection between railroads and industrial enterprises. The Standard Oil Company of New Jersey, for instance, owned or controlled a great many railroads. As a result of this, the Standard Oil Company received rebates which no one else could possibly hope to obtain. Because of those rebates, genuine competition among the companies was impossible.

They engaged also in "pooling" agreements. "Pooling" was a situation whereby independent units created a central administrative agency for the purpose of raising prices, or sometimes depressing prices. Such a practice was harmful to and resented by the users of railroad service.

All of these practices led to a political movement designed to curb the abuses of the railroad, a movement known as the Granger Movement. They led finally to the enactment in 1887 of the Interstate Commerce Act, which created the Interstate Commerce Commission. That Act contained some very simple prohibitions: it forbade excessive rates and gave to the I.C.C. some yardsticks by which the excessiveness of rates could be determined; it forbade discriminatory rates; and it forbade "pooling" by competing railroads. The prohibition of rate discrimination has since become the cornerstone of all transportation law, embodying the idea that a common carrier that holds itself out as providing service to everyone who needs such service must treat everybody alike. Anything else is a complete negation of the public obligation of such a calling. A common carrier is an enterprise which is impressed with the public interest, to put it in lawyers' terminology, and which therefore cannot be permitted to indulge in practices that might be countenanced if indulged in by ordinary private carriers.

This was the first real attempt at regulating business. It was an attempt which proceeded from the theory that competition between railroads (and this may be astonishing to those who know that railroads perhaps should have been regulated as natural monopolies) should be fostered but that certain abuses of competition should not be tolerated. The railroads, because of their monopoly position, were in a position to flout the necessities of ordinary competition.

But this action was not enough. The railroads were only one target of widespread public criticism. The trusts, too, were generally regarded as something evil that should be brought under control. A trust was a combination of firms which sought to escape the restraints, and avoid what they called the wastes of competition by absorbing, controlling, or forcing out of business all its would-be competitors. In other words, "if you can't beat them, join them"— by acting in concert with them in fixing prices and in dividing territories. The purpose of both trusts and pools is to get away from a competitive system of enterprise, and to impose a system which would not be competitive. Rather, it would be fixed and determined by the members of the trust or by the members of the pool.

The outcome of this was the passage of the Sherman Act in 1890. Senator Sherman, incidentally, was a native of Mansfield, Ohio, where his identification with the town may still be seen in a little sign at the city limits: "City of Mansfield, Home of Senator Sherman." The Sherman Act was a response to this movement of public opinion.

Laws in any free society originate not by imposition from above but in response to demands made by certain segments, or perhaps by the majority, of the people, with respect to problems which have arisen, abuses which cry for remedies, etc. The need at that time was that a means must be found to curb the abuses of concentrations of power. The only method which seemed consonant with traditions of law and philosophy, and which were consistent with political developments in Anglo-Saxon countries, was a direct statement that monopoly was frowned upon and that the market place should be regulated by competition.

In pursuance of this, the Sherman Act is extremely simple. It says in two paragraphs

that every contract, combination, or restraint of trade shall be illegal and punishable by fines and imprisonment, or that it shall be possible for the government to sue in equity, thus undo the consequences of such combination in restraint of trade; and

that every monopoly or every attempt at monopoly is illegal and subject to the same sanctions.

This Act is simple in that it provides something which cannot really be called regulation. Certainly, it cannot be called regulation in the sense in which the public utilities commission in Ohio or anywhere else, or even the Interstate Commerce Commission, regulates. There is no government agency which is continually saying to business what it must do and what it must not do. The control of the enforcement of the competitive policy which the Sherman Act embodies contemplates law suits. People from other countries have often said, and I think rightly so, that it is a peculiar American custom to confer upon the court power to resolve problems which in most other countries are resolved in some other way.

The idea conveyed by the Act is that the government, acting for the public interest, should pounce upon individual situations where anti-competitive behavior is found. The government should do it because private parties, in the majority of instances, cannot do it. Due to the time and expense involved, the enforcement of this policy could not be entrusted to private parties, lest it break down. Private parties may benefit from it, however, for private parties may bring suits for damages. After a government suit has been concluded, a private party may bring suit for damages against the same defendant, and the judgment in favor of the government is *prima facia* evidence. In other words, it may be said that the government has tried the case not only for its own benefit but for the benefit of private plaintiffs as well. It is a case-by-case enforcement.

Enforcement begins when a firm is accused of violating what I have called the Eleventh Commandment. What this really means can be determined only by a study of the cases. It is not an all-powerful governmental agency which sits on top of business and says, from day to day, that you must do this or not do that. The government, like the District Attorney with whom you are familiar in other cases, hails a party into court, saying to the court that this firm or that combination of firms has violated the rule that there must be competition rather than monopoly. It has violated the rule that competitors should not combine in restraint of trade.

The historical roots of this policy and procedure go back into the seventeenth century when England enacted a statute against monopoly, which resulted from resentment against the abuse of the power to grant monopolies that was at that time invested in the king.

Now, monopoly is the antithesis of competition. A monopolist does not have to worry about competition. He can control price, and he can see to it that no one will enter that particular business field. Competition is the opposite of monopoly, and the question may arise as to why we exalt competition. What is the good of a competitive enterprise? Why is it the keystone of our whole approach as reflected in our legal system? Are there any moral values to it? Are there any dangers in it that may give rise to immoral situations, to *unfair* competition? Why do we think that competition is a basic ingredient of American life?

Perhaps it should be said at the outset that the values of a competitive society are by no means only economic. The economic view is important, but it is not the only one. It has been said that the Sherman Act is the economic equivalent of the Due Process clause of the Constitution, that the Sherman Act is a charter of liberty. These three words, a "charter of liberty," were used by Senator Sherman in one of his concluding speeches in the United States Senate, when he pointed out that the Act is not a simple statute but a "charter of liberty." I urge you to keep that in mind. If we try to evaluate this idea of competition as the regulator of life, as the Eleventh Commandment to be enforced by courts, we must do so not merely from the point of view of economics, but also from the point of view of the "charter of liberty."

What is so good about competition? In a monopolistic society, you do not have freedom of opportunity. Here, all one has to do who thinks to pursue a calling, subject to the practicalities of the situation, is to persuade some banker to lend him the capital necessary for entering into the business. America has always been called the land of opportunity, but many people never stop to think what lies behind that often-pronounced phrase. A society in which there would be only one automobile manufacturer or only one steel manufacturer, etc., would not guarantee freedom or opportunity to go into the particular business which one feels qualified to pursue. Without freedom of opportunity a very essential attribute of the free enterprise society would disappear. This would present an awkward consequence, because the monopolist, who represents the opposite of freedom of opportunity, would not have any challenge to do better. To do better, in the economic sense, would be to cut costs and produce cheaper, and, secondly, to do better in the sense of innovating new products or improving existing ones and existing procedures, thereby assuring that the economy and all members of the community progress rather than stagnate.

The history of the Sherman Act enforcement is full of situations which illustrate this danger of monopoly and this benefit to be derived from freedom of opportunity, freedom for new people to enter. A case which illustrates this well is that involving the law suits against the Pullman Company some twenty years ago. The Pullman Company had monopolized the manufacture of sleeping cars and the servicing of sleeping cars. As a result, up to twenty years ago the sleeping cars available on American railroads were something awful to behold. One of the consequences of the law suit against Pullman was that when the stranglehold of Pullman— one of the very rare cases of a complete monopoly in the American economy—was broken, there appeared a great many enormously improved sleeping cars. Because they were more convenient, the old monstrosities disappeared. Such was the result of breaking up the monopoly.

The monopolist has an easy life because he has no spur to superior performance. The spur for superior performance, which incidentally is not limited to industrial enterprises, but is found also in academic and other human institutions, comes from competition. Progress is guaranteed by this idea of freedom of opportunity and the improvement that comes from it. In the monopolistic situation, the incentive for improvement is lacking.

Superior performance is the inevitable by-product of the competitive society as distinguished from both the monopolistic and the socialist society, because the incentive for superior performance may be weakened in a society where the major business units are owned by the state. This is one of the strongest reasons for our innate distrust of nationalized enterprises. Nationalization advocated by some in the transportation field may not solve anything.

The idea of incentive for superior performance has moral connotations of great significance, because it means that nobody should be permitted to rest on his oars, that nobody should be permitted to sleep, that nobody should be permitted to be lazy because his performance will not be challenged. There should be constant pressure for doing better, not merely for the purpose of accumulating greater profits, which, of course, is one of the incentives which are inevitable, but for creating a better life for all members of society. The profit motive seen in that context seems entirely unobjectionable, to put it mildly, from the point of view of both ethics and morality.

Still another area involving ethical considerations is that of pricing. The monopolist has complete control over price. Not being limited in any way by demand and supply, he may charge what the traffic will bear. From the social point of view, this is often harmful and undesirable. Even under competitive conditions which are not perfect—and most competition nowadays is not perfect—there is brought to bear upon the pricing process the rivalry between competitors: their constant striving to do better, to cut costs and prices, to pass on to consumers the benefits of more efficient operation. These are the socially beneficial results of competition. It leads to better performance and innovation, it keeps open the opportunity for new business entries, and it prevents price scalping of consumers.

All of this has political implications. A monopolist with complete power to exclude anyone from his line of endeavor, with complete control over price, with complete power to eliminate freedom of opportunity, with no incentive to do better, with a guarantee of the easy life at the expense of progress and therefore at the expense of the community—such a monopolist would acquire a degree of power that he would thereby automatically collide with basic economic and political postulates of American society. Without going into the philosophical basis of our Constitution, it is readily apparent that its framers had certain ideals in mind: that no branch of government should be all powerful, that the legislative and the executive branches should be subject to check by the judiciary, that the executive should be subject to check by the legislative, etc. This philosophy is built into the Constitution, which is devised in such a way as to prevent undue accumulation of power which could ultimately destroy these balances which are cherished by everyone.

There is a parallel construction in the business field. The monopolist constitutes such an accumulation of power as makes him unacceptable for both economic and political reasons. With such an accumulation of economic power, he might end up controlling society as a whole. In other words, the Sherman Act is one example in the economic field of the old American postulate which distrusts unlimited power. In a competitive society, unlimited power cannot exist.

V

THE SOCIETAL BASES OF ETHICS

Roscoe C. Hinkle

Introduction

Sociology's Concern with Ethics

As the discipline studying social behavior *as* social behavior, sociology has always been more or less directly concerned with the domain of ethics. Rules, their justifications, enforcement, conformity, and deviation are basic to the very existence of groups. Rules provide the foundation for organized, orderly social existence. They make it possible to anticipate, within limits, what others are likely to do and what we ought to do in relation to them under given circumstances. They make behavior predictable. All groups must and do have rules, even groups such as criminals.

From its very outset as a discipline, sociology has been concerned with moral or ethical phenomena. Auguste Comte, who is often regarded as its father, recognized that social stability and orderliness require common acceptance of moral beliefs. Probably the two most outstanding European sociologists of the late 19th and early 20th centuries, Emile Durkheim and Max Weber, were also fundamentally concerned with morality.

The Nature of Morality

Morality is indicated primarily by acceptance and observance of a certain kind of rules—moral rules. There are, of course, many kinds of rules. Technical and cognitive norms are illustrated in rules as to how to boil eggs, the most efficient way to manufacture TNT, etc. Aesthetic rules specify standards of taste, beauty, etc. Moral rules, however, are distinctive in that they define right, good, or appropriate conduct within and between groups. Although the sociologist is particularly interested in the conception of the moral as it is defined in our society and generally in Western European

51

civilization, he tries to avoid being circumscribed by the assumptions of his own social world.

In our society, the moral is signified by some prescriptive or proscriptive quality—some one of the many qualitatively different kinds of "shoulds" or "oughts." Yet, the sociologist is not likely to accept this quality as the exclusive criterion of the moral. Whatever is socially approved and the accepted is essentially the moral. The appropriate, the fitting, and the preferred are a part of the range of morality as well as the proper, prescribed, ordained, and sanctified. Thus, fashion, fad, convention, and etiquette entail morality as well as our mores. Similarly, the sociologist will likely be wary about universally imposing rationality and voluntarism as attributes of morality. Both the habitual and the affective may preponderate over the conscious, deliberate, and voluntary in moral conduct. Finally, the sociologist will also distinguish the proclaimed or professed morality as opposed to the operative morality.

Moral norms may vary in several aspects: their prevalence (how widely known, accepted, applicable); their manner of formulation (explicit *vs.* implicit, general *vs.* specific); their mode of enforcement (informal *vs.* formal, primacy of reward *vs.* primacy of punishment, range and intensity of rewards and punishments); their source of authority (divine revelation, wisdom of ancestors, ideas of natural law and inherent rights, charisma of leader, social expediency); their transmission (through primary groups *vs.* secondary groups); degree and kind of conformity required.

However, morality is not exclusively defined by the mere aggregate of concrete moral rules. It is evident also in what might be termed moral values which tend to be more general and abstract than the specific rules. A moral rule would be illustrated by the notion that everyone has a right to a certain level of public education or to vote. What these and other similar rules have in common is equalitarianism, a value. In American culture, progress, efficiency, achievement, freedom are values. As Robin Williams notes (in *American Society*, p. 374), values tend to have certain distinctive qualities: they are conceptual and abstract, affectively charged, are the criteria by which concrete goals are chosen, direct action, and signify important matters in a culture. Studies of values have become major preoccupations of sociologists (and other social scientists) during the last two decades. Large-scale projects have been undertaken at Harvard and Cornell Universities.

In brief, then, sociologists' studies of morality must involve investigations both of norms and values. Nevertheless, the sociological study of morality is itself nonevaluative. The sociologist is prohibited from being morally partisan. As a scientist, he cannot say that one society's judgment of what ought to be is better or more correct than another's.

Although a sociological study of the social and societal bases of ethics can be far-ranging, relevancy of the sociological study of morality for ethics in business can best be served by limiting this analysis to the following topics: a comparative, cross-societal and cross-cultural survey of ethics, especially morality in economic, economic-like, or economically-relevant situations; an examination of the rule of ethics in the organization of business enterprise in the Western world (Max Weber's thesis on the pertinence of the Protestant ethic for the "spirit of capitalism"); a consideration of ethics in American business enterprise, including the moral values of the (prospective) businessman (from the Cornell Value Study), and the impact of the larger societal context on ethics in business.

A Comparative, Cross-Societal and Cross-Cultural Survey of Morality in Economic, Economic-Like, or Economically-Relevant Situations

For materials outside of Western European societies, the sociologist tends to be compelled to go to the research of his anthropological colleagues. Yet, interpretation of the anthropological data requires that the sociologist be aware of the current arguments over ethical universalism-relativism. Unfortunately, the sociologist must also be aware of the different perspectives and emphases in the arguments.

The proponents of ethical universalism tend to look for types of abstractly similar social situations subject to moral norms. This would seem to be the position of such anthropologists as Redfield,

Bidney, Kluckhohn, and Linton, for example. As an illustration, we may note Linton's emphasis on the universality of sex behavior (incest, rape, pre-marital and extra-marital relations), responsibilities of members of the family toward one another (spouse-spouse, parent-child, sibling-sibling), some recognition of personal property, the notion that the interests of the society become paramount to those of the individual at some point, the demand for truth in certain areas of personal interaction, etc.

However, the proponents of ethical relativism focus on the study of the content of the operating rules in social situations. They are concerned with what is specifically required or approved, who has what rights and duties, what circumstances qualify the application of the rules, etc.

For example, it is said: "Just as our more or less literate children today all know that the Eskimo rub noses as a sign of greeting and affection, so we—their more sophisticated elders—know that Eskimo ideas of marital fidelity are different from our own, that they exchange wives freely, lending bed and wife with equal hospitality to visiting friends" (as part of the husband's obligations to his guests).[1]

Also, we know that "contraventions of our attitudes—to adultery, or truth-telling or killing or toward virtually any rule we accept —are extremely common among the peoples of different cultures of the world. We know that not all people are shocked or indignant at the things which shock us"[2]

"A little less confidently, we realize that they may instead be shocked at some aspects of our behavior which seem to us either desirable, or natural and morally neutral"—such as permitting old people to waste away and die from painful diseases, or failing to share our daily bread with all our needy friends and neighbors.[3]

For example, "In some Plains Indians languages, the possessive pronoun is not used with such words as 'bread'; it is inconceivable to them that anyone should consider food something for his own private consuming. One may own other things—valuables such as

[1] Edel, May and Abraham, *Anthropology and Ethics*, p. 19.
[2] *Ibid.*, p. 19.
[3] *Ibid.*, p. 19.

horses, for example—but food is for sharing. To the Indian agent struggling with problems of distributing flour rations, there is only improvidence in the Indian habit of sharing the goods received among any of his kinsmen who choose to lay claim to his help."[4]

Among the Eskimo, the successful hunter has absolute property rights over his kill and this "is regarded as right and proper." But there is also a notion of generosity which is likely to incline him to share with those of his neighbors who are needy. He will get both "the personal satisfaction of being the important man who has helped everyone out, and a considerable measure of social insurance (the people with whom he shares may later share with him)."[5] Such beneficence was applauded but not required.

Among the Australians, sharing was accomplished through the specific kinship obligations which the hunter had to others rather than by a separate generalized norm. "Instead of the hunter giving freely of his surplus, he divides the game he kills according to absolutely required rules . . . . (among) his grandfather, his paternal uncle, his father and his father-in-law, and so on. These (shares) are not gifts; they are their absolute due."[6]

"Melanesian hunters in some areas must give away all the products of their hunting—not out of a streak of queer generosity, but because their eating of them is prohibited by a tabu bringing terrible consequences in its train."[7]

Thus, there are "societies where to eat your own crops, grown in your own garden, or the game bagged by your own hunting efforts, is out of the question, wrong in all the ways in which stealing is wrong with our own morality—offensive to gods and men, indicative of a generally bad character, ringed around with evil consequences both social and supernatural—in short, a form of wickedness so wrong for the average man it is not usually even an admitted temptation. There are societies in which it is required that you eat your deceased friend or brother to show your respect for him; others in which a cannibal feast on an enemy is an every-

[4] *Ibid.*, pp. 71-72.
[5] *Ibid.*, p. 74.
[6] *Ibid.*, p. 74.
[7] *Ibid.*, p. 75.

day event, and supplying this special game for the larder is a required mark of adult status."[8]

Honesty and promptness in meeting obligations in trading relations vary. "Among the Trobriand islanders of the South Pacific a basic mode of mutual obligation is so ingrained that a man will abandon a day's highly paid pearl diving for a puzzled white trader in order to do a day's fishing for an inland neighbor in return for a few yams or other farm produce, because the obligation to a trading partner must always be fulfilled. But their neighbors from the nearby island of Dobu who also live by a complicated system of trade relations, consider any cheating one can actually get away with as a mark of the greatest shrewdness, an admired stepping-stone to success."[9]

"Anthropologists have found that differences go far beyond these matters of specific rules and regulations, or even goals and values. There are different kinds of sanctions to support moral codes. In one society shame and ridicule may be open weapons, and public opinion a high charged deterrent pressure, while in another, a man's neighbors will be very little concerned with his breaches of the moral code, shrugging them off with 'Well, what can you do? That's just the kind of man he happens to be.' There are differences in the systematizations, the justifications, and rationalizations which people use, and in the basic values and world attitudes which underlie or elaborate their codes. Some people have gods who are malicious and unconcerned with human morals, while others worship supernaturals who have the same kind of concern with man's behavior that we traditionally consider appropriate. For some people, moral issues are explicit, verbalized, central; for others, seldom the conscious center in decision situations. The structure of conscience itself, it now begins to appear, may not be quite the same for all people; perhaps some mechanisms of pure fear and prudence, a total lack of concern with any internal goals and standards may be the picture for at least some of the societies in the world."[10]

8 *Ibid.*, p. 20.
9 *Ibid.*, p. 21.
10 *Ibid.*, pp. 21-22.

A Consideration of the Moral Values of the American Businessman

Several sources may be used to attempt to infer the morality of the American businessman: studies of the upper class in American society (which presumably includes the corporate magnate); studies of white collar crime or illegalities; and studies of the values of the prospective businessman.

All of these sources do have their liabilities. Both the upper class and white collar illegalities researches require considerable conjecture. Our social class analyses, ordinarily, have not separated out the moral values of American businessmen as opposed to American professionals. It is also rather obviously difficult to judge what the ethics of the American businessman are through certain classes of illegalities, whose rate of occurrence is difficult, if not impossible, to establish. Finally, the studies of prospective businessmen are limited by virtue of the fact that we do not know how many of such individuals actually did become businessmen. Nevertheless, Morris Rosenberg's *Occupations and Values* is a provocative study, which does merit scrutiny. The Rosenberg research was part of the Cornell Values Study, which was based on a study of a representative sample of 2,758 students at Cornell in 1950, and 4,858 students at Cornell, Dartmouth, Fisk, Harvard, Michigan, North Carolina, U.C.L.A., Wayne, Wesleyan, and Yale in 1952.

Predominant Value-Complex of Students Selecting Business-Related Occupations

By means of a weighted average, each occupation was ranked in terms of the emphasis which people planning to enter the field placed on the three major value-complexes: self-expression-oriented —permits individual to be creative and original, to use his special abilities and aptitudes; people-oriented—permits individual to be helpful to others, work with people rather than things; extrinsic reward-oriented—provides individual status and prestige; chance to earn good deal of money; stable, secure future.

People planning to enter real estate or finance, sales-promotion, hotel management, law, advertising, and business place the greatest stress on the extrinsic rewards of money, status, and security (3.64, 3.58, 3.53, 3.34, 3.21, 3.19 and for security 2.30, 2.60, 2.39, 2.16, 2.18, 2.30).[11] Conversely, most of these occupations tended to fall at the bottom of the self-expression-oriented complex (beginning at the bottom, sales-promotion, 3.20; hotel-food, 3.23; real estate-finance, 3.52; personnel, 3.59 (government, 3.69); business-unspecified, 3.71).[12] And, interestingly, law, sales-promotion, advertising-public relations, real estate-finance, hotel-food (journalism-drama), and business-unspecified fall in the middle of the occupational ranking for the people-oriented value complex.[13]

Faith in People and Occupation

Using five items, Rosenberg constructed a scale of faith in people (or human nature) and made an analysis of occupational placement. He found that in the rank ordering of occupations social work, personnel work, and teaching were at the top, and advertising-public relations, business-finance, and sales-promotion were at the bottom of "high faith in people." For "medium and low faith in people," the reverse held true.[14]

Furthermore, of the students with "high" faith in people, only 2 per cent would pick as their first criterion for selecting an occupation "a chance to earn a good deal of money." But almost 20 per cent of the students with low faith in people would pick as their first criterion for selecting an occupation "a chance to earn a good deal of money." Conversely, of the students with a high faith in people, 25 per cent would give a minimal emphasis to selecting a job on the basis of promise of monetary return; and of students with a low faith in people, only 8 per cent would give a minimal emphasis to selecting a job on the basis of monetary return.[15]

Rosenberg also attempted an occupational comparison of students with high faith in people and people-oriented values with students who have low faith in people and who select money as a primary occupational criterion. Of the individuals who have high

[11] Rosenberg, Morris, *Occupations and Values*, p. 19.
[12] *Ibid.*, p. 17.
[13] *Ibid.*, p. 18.
[14] *Ibid.*, p. 27.
[15] *Ibid.*, p. 29.

faith in people and who hold people-oriented values, 50 per cent choose teaching, social work, and personnel work. Of the individuals who have low faith in people and who subscribe to a monetary value of the job, only 8 per cent choose the previous three occupations. Only 3 per cent of those with a high faith in people and people-oriented values selected business, real estate-finance, sales-promotion and advertising-public relations. Twenty-three per cent of students with low faith in people and with a high monetary emphasis in selection of an occupation do prefer the occupations just mentioned. What seems to be the more important is the pattern of avoidance and not the pattern of selection. The persons with high faith in people and people-oriented values tend to avoid business, real estate-finance, sales-promotion and advertising-public relations. The low-faith and monetarily oriented tend to avoid teaching, social work, and personnel work.

Consequences for Ethics of Social Change of American Society Toward a More Urban, Mass Society

Moral Rules and Social Control in a Changing Society

Americans are increasingly living within social relationships which were unanticipated and unregulated by the historic precepts of the religious traditions in Western European civilization. This statement does not assert that the moral precepts as handed down in the Judaic-Christian tradition are irrelevant or inapplicable. It means that the Old and New Testament prescriptions of right conduct presupposed an agrarian, primary group society.

The Old Testament is filled with directives as to how one is to treat one's wife, children, servants, and neighbors in specific situations. Christ's doctrine of brotherly love was a generalized precept but He also spoke in parables, to enlarge its meaning. The duties of servant and master are spelled out, those of wife and husband, neighbor and neighbor, adults and children.

The great religions arose in the desert, centuries ago, where social relationships were well-nigh confined to the kin group and the small cohesive neighborhood. It would seem significant that Christ's only statement about secondary-group relationships came in His cryptic answer to the Pharisees who sought to trap Him in a charge of treason: "Render unto Caesar the things which are Caesar's; and unto God the things which are God's." And the things that were Caesar's in the early Christian era were few and, for the most part, remote from the primary-group life and problems of that era.

The modern social order is composed of much more powerful and ramified bureaucracies than those of the Roman legions, procurators, and tax gatherers. Caesar is no longer one but many (union and trade association, government, armed services, police and courts, federal bureaus, various medical associations, farm bureau, N.A.M., U.N., and many others). Neither the Old nor the New Testament specifies rights and duties in the secondary, bureaucratic context.

The duty of the husbandman to his hired hand was—perhaps still is—plain. But the duty of a group of corporation directors to their 50,000 factory employees, who live and work in cities distant from the directors' conference table, is perhaps not as plain and certainly not specified in Holy Writ. It can be derived, but not incontestably. And this, indeed, is the whole point of the social world in which we live—our moral rules have to be derived or translated from an agrarian or even nomadic primary group.

It is not only that modern society provides a whole panorama of groups and social relationships which were unanticipated by and undefined by the rules of an agrarian, primary group society, but that urban society also presents social conditions which render primary group social controls less effective. Conscience, gossip, rumor, wit and humor, ridicule, verbal commendation, withdrawal and shunning can effectively maintain moral rules as represented by folkways and mores. However, these informal controls are effective for a society as a whole only if it is communal, folk, or primary group in character. All of the members must be in close physical proximity, face-to-face association. Thus, the membership must be relatively small in numbers so that they can know one another personally. This intimacy, in turn, is linked with frequent, intense, durable social relationships. Relationships tend to be personal and personalized and inclusive.

The very roles they play include many aspects of behavior rather than merely some limited segment of the individual's activities. This inclusiveness also means that members interact with one another in a wide variety of contexts. Each person tends to know others both extensively and intensively, and thus each person is sensitive to the judgments of others. Conformity through these informal controls also tends to be relatively insured because persons conceive of other individuals and the social relations as intrinsically rather than instrumentally important. They are valued for themselves rather than as means to other ends. Conformity tends to be effective via these controls because members' ends tend to interpenetrate. They have similar desires and attitudes so that they are striving for similar things and can be together without disagreement. This sharing of ends and the similarity of experience tends also to facilitate a strong sense of solidarity and identification among the members so that what one member tends to experience another also experiences (empathically or sympathetically).

Relationships within the context are typically different, however, with important consequences for social control. The contacts that individuals make as they go about their daily lives in the metropolis are great in number, many are fleeting, even though face-to-face, and of the touch-and-go variety, and many are only indirect (mechanically visual or auditory). People associate constantly with hundreds or possibly even thousands of persons, often in close quarters, but the contacts are either with complete strangers or with persons with whom they have only occasional contact and very limited acquaintance. One is tied to few persons by gossip and the sharing of experience. Relationships are anonymous, depersonalized, and specialized or segmental. Most of those with whom you have contact have an interest in you and you in them, which is limited to the narrow task or transaction at hand. Individuals are emotionally detached; they only know small parts of other persons by virtue of their segmental roles. Perhaps the case could hardly be otherwise. A genuine personal relationship with the thousands with whom one comes in daily contact would be as physically exhausting as it would be physically impossible.

Such relationships do not make for solidarity and mutual understanding. They are conducive to individuation, indifference to others, reserve, and a superficial tolerance of anything that does not affect the given individual immediately in an adverse fashion. These relationships render primary or informal controls relatively ineffective. Anonymity, impersonality, segmental roles, social distance destroy the bases on which informal, primary group controls can operate. People are not effectively controlled in direct contacts when in a real sense they have no personal reputation to maintain. The impersonality, anonymity, and individuation, the physical and social mobility of the urban population, the social distance and strangeness of persons with respect to one another, and the general complexity of relationships in the metropolis do not permit gossip, rumor, wit, ridicule, verbal commendation, withdrawal and shunning—the primary group controls—to operate effectively in the interests of general social order. Individuals tend to have no personal reputations to maintain and no informal controls to make them operate that way. Furthermore, there is a great variety of standards of behavior, often of a conflicting nature, to choose among. At the same time, the social situations requiring control increase in kind, gravity, and number.

This means that the sanctions of social behavior must be formulated in terms of formal controls. And such controls tend to operate within the large-scale bureaucratic organizations and between them. Within the organization, informal controls may indeed operate effectively only within the ambit of direct and persistent social interaction, as in the office of a department or a particular sector of a plant. But by-and-large primary group sentiment and solidarity do not tie together the organization as a whole, and thus specific rules and regulations are demanded; they state what constitute infractions of rules, what the penalties are and establish specific roles to police conformity, and specific roles to determine guilt of violations and penalties. Every large-scale organization tends to operate this way. The same kind of formal system is active across and between different organizations. However, it has the peculiar political, jurisdictional status we call law, administered through the coercive power political agencies, especially police force and the court system.

The Moral Consequences of a Mass Society[16]

Mass production and mass consumption of the mass society have accentuated the materialization and pecuniarization of values. Unwittingly, the ascetic elements of Christianity have been undermined. Early Protestantism was characteristically ascetic. Early Protestantism tended to center around a stress on asceticism with stress on self-denial and self-discipline. Fun and enjoyment were identified with carnal pleasures, with the things of the flesh. And, accordingly—lest we forget—many of the early Protestant sects banned smoking, drinking, dancing, card playing, wearing of jewelry, etc.

Although Calvanistic Protestantism may have been critically important in the development of the disciplined work ethic and productivity of early capitalism, its retention of asceticism is hardly congruent with a mass consumption-oriented society. Thus, the success of advertisement and amusement with gratification seems clearly to have come at the expense of, indeed, with the undermining of, the asceticism. (Not all of the moral resistance to gratificatory consumption has disappeared and motivation research is doing its best to circumvent, if not to destroy, these last obstacles.)

Most Americans have absorbed the goal of material success and material gratification. They cannot conceive of activity without some reward in fun or self-gratification. Paradoxically, increasing mechanization of the productive process causes those who are directly involved to experience ennui and alienation, while at the same time it causes men to be oriented only to monetary reward and to seek release and expression via gratificatory relaxation and consumption. The cycle of work and vacation (and the content of vacations), the shift in popular literature from heroes of production to heroes of consumption, the content of popular songs, and the transition from holy days to holidays attest to the advent of mass gratification via mass consumption.

More than ever, values are being reduced to or translated into the value of money and the things money can buy. "I've been rich and I've been poor," Sophie Tucker has said, "and, believe me,

[16] This section is especially indebted to C. Wright Mills' *The Power Elite* and *White Collar*.

rich is best." As C. Wright Mills remarks, "the question for Americans" is "not 'is there anything that money, used with intelligence, will not buy?' but, 'how many of the things that money will not buy are desired more than what money will buy?' Money is the one unambiguous criterion of success, and such success is still the sovereign American value. . . . . In a society in which the money-maker has had no serious rival for repute and honor, the word 'practical' comes to mean useful for private gain, and 'common sense,' the sense to get ahead financially. The pursuit of the moneyed life is the commanding value, in relation to which the influence of other values has declined. . . . ."[17]

Much of American corruption, associated with the effort to become rich and then richer, reflects the social condition which Emile Durkheim termed anomie, normlessness. In the case of American corruption, the anomie—as Robert Merton has argued—obtains from a strong stress on a cultural goal, material and monetary success, without a corresponding emphasis on the rules by which money is acquired and used.

On the one hand, the advent of secondary relations provides circumstances which are not immediately definable by our earlier moral codes and renders the traditional informal controls relatively ineffective, and on the other, the power afforded to top office holders in the centralized administrations of the bureaucracies, along with the interlinkage and centralization of political institutions and economic opportunities, mean that both the new rules of an impersonal social world and the formalized controls to support these rules often do not work effectively.

As C. Wright Mills notes: "Many little disclosures, spurring the moral worry of those still capable of such concern, indicate how widespread public immorality might be."[18] The broad acceptance of material and monetary values, the complexity of the division of labor, the hidden and anonymous character of much of decision, the interconnections and centralization of economic and political bureaucracies, plus the power, influence, and prestige of their top office holders mean that corruption can continue at the top of

[17] Mills, C. Wright, *The Power Elite*, p. 346.
[18] *Ibid.*, p. 339-341.

American life without serious deterrents. There "is the feeling that the bigger you are, the less likely you are to be caught. . . . . There is the feeling that all the petty cases seem to signify something grander, that they go deeper and that their roots are now well organized in the higher and middle American ways of life. But among the mass distractions this feeling soon passes harmlessly away. For the American distrust of the high and mighty is a distrust without doctrine and without political focus; it is a distrust felt by the mass as a series of more or less cynically expected disclosures. Corruption and immoralities, petty and grand, are facts about higher circles, often even characteristic facts about many of them. But the immoral tone of American society today also involves the lack of public sensibility when confronted with these facts. Effective moral indignation is not evoked by the corrupt public life of our time . . . ."[19]

The effort to subject the expense account to more rigorous scrutiny and to require the withholding of taxes on dividends has encountered vigorous, if not violent, opposition from the higher circles of American life. Mills has acridly remarked, "High income taxes have resulted in a network of collusions between big firm and higher employee. There are many ingenious ways to cheat the spirit of the tax laws . . . . and the standards of consumption of many high-priced men are determined more by complicated expense accounts than by simple take-home pay. Like prohibition, the laws of income taxes and the regulations of wartime exist without the support of firm business convention. It is merely illegal to cheat them, but it is smart to get away with it.[20]

"A society that narrows the meaning of 'success' to the big money and in its terms condemns failure as the chief vice, raising money to the plane of absolute value, will produce the sharp operator and the shady deal. Blessed are the cynical for only they have what it takes to succeed."[21]

"Mass production and mass consumption have also transformed the ego into an instrument of salesmanship. Personality has become

[19] Ibid., p. 341.
[20] Ibid., p. 347.
[21] Ibid., p. 347.

a means of manipulation. The successful person makes an instrument of his own appearance and personality. The smile becomes a commercialized lure. Kindness and friendliness are devices to disarm the unwary. Sincerity is detrimental to one's job, until the rules of salesmanship and business become a genuine aspect of oneself. Tact is a series of little lies about one's own feelings, until one is emptied of such feelings."[22]

Each person needs to become a quick "character analyst." If the other individual is phlegmatic, he should be handled deliberately; if he is sensitive, he should be handled with directness; if opinionated, with deference; if openminded, with frankness; if cautious, handle him with proof.[23]

Vocationally, personality often actually replaces skill as a requirement: a personable appearance is emphasized as being more important in success and advancement than experience or skill or intelligence. In a recent study of graduates of Purdue University, "better intelligence paid only $150.00 a year bonuses, while personality paid more than six times that much in return for the same period and with the same men. Corporate business has recognized the role of "effective personalities" and many have sponsored courses for their white-collar personnel. Dale Carnegie's classic and his courses have become almost a tradition.

From the areas of salesmanship proper, "the requirements of personality market have diffused as style of life. What began as the public and commercial relations of business have become deeply personal: there is a public relations aspect to private relations of all sorts, including even relations with one's self. The new ways are diffused by charm and success schools and by best-seller literature. The sales personality, built and maintained for operation on the personality market, has become a dominating type, a pervasive model for imitation for masses of people, in and out of selling. The literature of self-improvement has generalized the traits and tactics of salesmanship for the population at large."[24]

The success literature still focuses "upon personal virtues, but they are not the sober virtues once imputed to successful entre-

[22] Mills, C. Wright, *White Collar*, p. 183.
[23] *Ibid.*, p. 185.
[24] *Ibid.*, p. 187.

preneurs. Now the stress is on agility rather than ability, on 'getting along' in a context of associates, superiors, and rules rather than 'getting ahead' across an open market; on whom you know rather than what you know; on techniques of self-display and the generalized knack of handling people, rather than on moral integrity, substantive accomplishments, and solidity of person; on loyalty to, or even identity with, one's own firm, rather than entrepreneurial virtuosity."[25]

Yet it is the sale and manipulation of personality that "underlies the all-pervasive distrust and self-alienation so characteristic of metropolitan people. . . . . People are required by the salesman ethic and convention to pretend interest in others in order to manipulate them. This ethic is conformed to as part of one's job and one's style of life, but with a winking eye, for one knows that manipulation is inherent in every human contact. Men are estranged from one another as each secretly tries to make an instrument of the other, and in time a full circle is made: one makes an instrument of himself, and is estranged from it also."[26]

The other prevalent feature of mass society, mass communications, is perhaps even more important in its ethical consequences than are mass production, mass distribution, and mass consumption. Mills is convinced that the mass media are crucially important in transforming society into media markets in mass-like society, with a higher ratio of deliverers of opinion to receivers, the decreased chance to answer back effectively, the violent banalization and stereotyping of our very sense organs in terms of which the media compete for attention. The media have superceded first-hand experience so that they guide our very experience by setting standards of credulity and reality. They tend to get the individual to respond in terms of stereotypes. In responding in terms of stereotypes the individual gains the good solid feeling of being correct without having to think.

The mass media, especially television, often encroach upon small-scale discussion and destroy the chance for reasonable, leisurely, human interchange of opinion. They destroy privacy. They neither

[25] *Ibid.*, p. 263.
[26] *Ibid.*, p. 187-188.

enable the individual to transcend his narrow milieu nor clarify its private meaning. They do not enable the listener or the viewer truly to connect his daily life with the larger realities of the world. Rather, they distract the individual and obscure his chance to understand himself or his world, by fastening his attention on artificial frenzies that are resolved within the program framework, usually by violent action or by what is called humor. The animated distraction is a tension between the wanting and not having of commodities or of woman held to be good-looking—this suspended agitation goes nowhere.

The program contents (especially TV, radio, movies) are geared not to stimulate reflection and comparison. People are not provoked to search for counter-statements. Even if they attempted, they could scarcely succeed, for the media do not offer genuine competition. The apparent variety and competition are more in terms of variations on a few standardized themes than of clashing issues. The freedom to raise issues effectively seems more and more confined to those interests that have ready and continued access to the media. In fact, the mass media disfavor those who are against things. They trivialize issues into personal squabbles. They mirror the popular images of individual success in achieving individual goals. Egoism is emphasized. But by contrast there is no emphasis on collective adventure. The social basis of problems is ignored. Political meanings are not examined in the mass media. Politics are trivialized with the prevailing clichés or immoralized as the doings of bad men.

Whether intended or not, the nonpolitical or false political content is congruent with the conceptions and values of owners and directors, whose interests are served by presentation of individual success stories rather than the facts of collective success and tragedies.

For Mills the most significant thing about the media is their function for manipulation at the disposal of the elites of wealth and power. Newspapers, radio, and television are all interlocked in operations. In 1959, only 42 U.S. cities had competing newspapers, while the remaining 1,600 were either one-newspaper towns or had two newspapers under a single management. And one-fourth of our newspaper circulation is attained by a few newspaper chains.

Most of the news that reaches the print passes through one of the two major newsgathering services—the Associated Press, a cooperative to which most papers belong; the U.P.I., affiliated with Scripps-Howard and Hearst chains.

The total picture of the press is one that is far from freely competitive in the traditional sense, yet is far from a complete monopoly. The degree of concentration in the industry vests in a relatively small number of persons a great power to determine what shall reach the presses.

Because the FCC limits the number of stations a person or company may own, concentration in radio rests more on network affiliation and program sponsorship than on station ownership. Practically, most stations belong to one of the four networks whose shows occupy the good listening hours. Since network broadcasts tend to be sponsored by advertisers, the advertisers control broadcasting in a literal sense: the advertising agency not only supplies the commercial but supplies the entire show, with the station operator merely a supplier of radio time. A few large advertisers, operating through a still smaller number of advertising agencies, supply the bulk of network income. A 1959 study found that over 90 per cent of all broadcasting during prime evening hours originated with two networks and the nine stations they own and operate. Incidentally, the FCC's effort to infuse new blood into radio by FM licensing failed because of industry opposition. Most of the FM licenses are now held by operators of AM stations.

When television arrived, the established broadcasters with their competitive advantages tended to take over licenses. The 1957 study by the FCC revealed that in the top 25 market areas of the country, 71 per cent of the TV stations were held in multiple ownership (several stations owned by a single owner), 20 per cent by newspapers, and only 9 per cent by single independent owners.

As a whole, nearly one-third of the radio and television stations are today affiliated with newspapers under common ownership or control. In over one-third of the cities with only one radio station, that station is associated with the only newspaper, giving an absolute monopoly of local news. No one is accusing the owners and managers of the mass media of conspiratorial designs. Such control as they have was gained to enhance profits and not to enforce ideological uniformity. But the result might be the same.

What disturbs some intellectuals is that this situation allows manipulation in behalf of members of the top circle of American life. The higher agents of these media are themselves either among the elite of American life or are very important among their servants. "Manipulation becomes a problem wherever men have power that is concentrated and willful but do not have authority, or when, for any reason, they do not wish to use their power openly. Then the powerful seek to rule without showing their powerfulness. They want to rule, as it were, secretly, without publicized legitimation. It is in this mixed case—as in the intermediate reality of the American today—that manipulation is a prime way of exercising power. Small circles of men are making decisions which they need to have at least authorized by indifferent or recalcitrant people over whom they do not exercise explicit authority, legitimate and voluntarily obeyed. So the small circle tries to manipulate these people into willing acceptance or cheerful support of their decisions or opinions —or at least to the rejection of possible counter-opinions."[27]

The power situation in the contemporary period is quite different from what it was in the pre-capitalist era. Then it was known and personal. The responses were directed to known and concrete targets. But in an impersonalized and more anonymous system of control, explicit responses are not possible: anxiety is likely to replace fear; insecurity, to replace worry. The foci of power are unknown. Targets for revolt are not readily available. Symbols in terms of which to challenge power are not available. As political power has been centralized, the issues professionalized and compromised by the two-party state, a sort of impersonal manipulation has replaced authority. Manipulation arises when there is a centralization of power that is not publicly justified. Decisions are hidden. Manipulation feeds upon and is fed by mass indifference. No symbols or principles are argued over and debated in public. Insecurity and striving are not attached to political symbols, but are drained off by the distractions of amusement, the frenzied search for commodities, or turned in upon the self as busy little frustrations. There is no organ-

[27] Mills, C. Wright, *The Power Elite*, p. 317.

ized effort in American society to develop common consciousness of common interests. Though political institutions are objectively more important in the course of American history because of increased and centralized power, there is less and less subjective interest to the population at large because of mass alienation.[28]

The development of the metropolis, the community center of mass society, has had a number of consequences. It contributes to the formulation of a mass society by segregating men and women into narrowed routines and environment. They have no firm sense of integrity as a public. They know one another only as fractions in specialized milieux rather than in the fullness of the convergences of life routines as in the publics of small communities. In the division of labor, too, the jobs of men are more or less narrow milieux and the positions from which a view of the productive process as a whole can be had are centralized, as men are alienated not only from the product and the tools of their labor, but from any understanding of the structure and processes or production. Prejudgement and stereotype flourish. Clashes of viewpoint are not genuinely experienced or, if so, only as rudeness. There is an isolating blaséness of metropolitan life. Each group, each class, is trapped by its confining circle. The one-class suburbs are cut off from differences. Thus, the city is a structure composed of such little environments, and each set of inhabitants is cut off from the other sets.

"On the one hand, there is the increased scale and centralization of the structure of decision; and on the other, the increasingly narrow sorting out of men into milieux. From both sides, there is the increased dependence upon the formal media of communication, including those of education itself. But the man in the mass does not gain a transcending view from the media; instead he gets his experience stereotyped, and then he gets sunk further by that experience. He cannot detach himself in order to observe, much less to evaluate, what he is experiencing, much less what he is not experiencing."[29] He fulfills only the routines that exist. He has lost the desire to be independent; he merely wants to get his share of what is around with as little trouble as he can and with as much fun as possible. He is

---

[28] Mills, C. Wright, *White Collar*, p. 348-350.
[29] Mills, C. Wright, *The Power Elite*, p. 322.

not self-conscious; his desires are insinuated into him. Life "in a society of masses implants insecurity and further impotence; it makes men uneasy and vaguely anxious; it isolates the individual from the solid group; it destroys firm group standards. Acting without goals, the man in the mass just feels pointless."[30]

Political and social apathy, alienation, estrangement are the joint consequence of the character of mass communications and the metropolis. There is indeed a direct relation between powerlessness felt and low occupation status, low educational attainment, and low income. In an impersonalized and anonymous system of control, anxiety is more likely to be a response than explicit fear; insecurity more likely than worry. The problem is who really has power, for often the tangled and hidden system seems a complex yet organized irresponsibility. Targets for revolt, given the will to revolt, are not readily available. In the narrow range of assertion and counter-assertion and trivialization of politics in the mass media, insecurity and striving are not attached to political symbols, but are drained off by the distractions of amusement, the frenzied search for commodities, or turned in upon the self as busy little frustrations. Men feel distant from events and powerless to order them.

Even those who vote are not necessarily politically involved. In the majority of cases voting is in terms of a family tradition of political preference. Voting does not typically involve political expectations of great moment, and such demands as are entailed are formalized and unconnected with personal troubles. Furthermore, often little more than 50 per cent of the eligibles do vote.

Consequences of the Mechanization and Bureaucratization of Business Organization

There is a meaninglessness to physical or manual work. As opposed to 85 per cent of professionals and executives who claim their work is interesting and enjoyable, only 41 per cent of factory workers make a similar judgment.[31]

Under modern conditions, the direct technical processes of work have been declining in meaning for the mass of employees. Work

[30] *Ibid.*, p. 323.
[31] Mills, C. Wright, *White Collar*, p. 229.

lacks intrinsic meaning. Simultaneously, income, power, and status have come to the fore as sources of extrinsic meaning. Alienation of man from both product and process of work is entailed by the legal framework of modern capitalism and the modern division of labor. The worker does not own the product or the tools of his production. In the labor contract he sells his time, energy, and skill, or even personality into the power of others. His work life comes under the control of others. The level of skills and the areas in which independent judgment are permitted are subject increasingly to the management of others. The intricate division of labor does not allow the individual to perceive the work in its role in the total technical process. It loses meaning. Except for those at the top of the organizational hierarchy, rationality has been expropriated from work and any total view and understanding of its process.

Alienation from work has introduced the sharp split between work and leisure. "The necessity to work and alienation from work make it a grind and the more grind there is, the more need to find relief in the jumpy or dreamy models available in modern mass leisure."[32] Leisure time comes to mean an unserious freedom from the authoritarian seriousness of the job. But some critics claim that modern leisure only diverts man, does not calm or relax him, from the restless grind.

There is also bureaucratic impersonality and loss of responsibility. Large-scale organization induces impersonality and impersonality makes it difficult to fix responsibility. Decisions tend to be announced in the name of the organization or department or office; their sources are not readily or easily identifiable. Bureaucratic authority tends to remove decision making from the lower rungs of the bureaucratic ladder. Unquestioning acquiescence is demanded; this is part of the division of labor; decision making is management's prerogative. But to the extent that the person working on the plant floor feels divorced from the decision-making process, to that extent he is likely to feel relieved of responsibility. Initiative is lost. The fact that decision making is associated with the top of the bureaucratic hierarchy means that the legitimation of initiative for those at the bottom is removed. Those in intermediate ranks tend

[32] *Ibid.*, p. 237.

to play it safe by meticulous observance of rules and regulations. Functionaries tend to be rewarded for their conformity. And, generally, the longer the functionary remains with the organization, the greater the stake in timidity and conservatism. He will avoid infringement on the prerogatives of his superiors. Initiative goes.

VI

THE PROTESTANT ETHIC AND ECONOMIC BEHAVIOR

CHRISTEN T. JONASSEN

Ethical problems are concerned with what is right and wrong, with what is blameworthy or praiseworthy, and with what is desirable and undesirable. When, therefore, we discuss "Societal Bases of Ethics," with relation to business, we deal with the origin of a system of social prescriptions through which social legitimization is achieved for certain types of economic behavior.

There is probably no single work concerning the social foundations of the ethics of economic activity which has stimulated as much discussion as has Max Weber's *The Protestant Ethic and the Spirit of Capitalism*.[1] Weber's theory about the influence of Protestantism on economic life is still very much a live issue today after a half century of learned and sometimes acrimonious debate. The thesis that ascetic Protestantism, and especially Puritanism, created a climate of ideas and stimulated motivations that greatly facilitated the development of capitalism has continued to be of interest because it concerns the very foundations of western culture and focuses on the ideological, political and economic struggle which divides the world today and which threatens mankind with annihilation. In a sense, Weber's thesis, since it stresses spiritual variables as causal factors, poses an anti-thesis to that of Marx which emphasizes materialistic factors in accounting for economic behavior and the ideology that governs it. The latter would hold that the Protestant Ethic was merely a superstructure of ideas determined by its adherents' relationship to the means of production, while Weber saw Puritanism as a system of ideas and values that facilitated, if not

---

[1] *Die Protestantische Ethik und der Geist des Kapitalismus* was first published in the *Archiv fur Sozialwissenschaft und Sozialpolitik,* Vol. XX, XXI, 1904-5. It was translated by Talcott Parsons, *The Protestant Ethic and the Spirit of Capitalism* (New York: Charles Scribner's Sons), 1930.

determined, the development of the modern capitalistic economic system.

Weber's assumption that there existed a close relationship between Protestantism, capitalism and economic progress was based on his observation that in states of mixed religious faith, it was Protestants, and in wholly Protestant states, Puritan sects who achieved marked success in such enterprises. He also found that Protestant groups to a greater extent than others in the population engaged in economic enterprises contributing to industrial and capitalistic expansion. He furthermore held that after the Reformation economic progress was more rapid in Protestant countries and particularly in countries where a Calvinist type of religion predominated. There was apparently something about Protestantism which created values, motivation, and life habits which were conducive to capitalistic enterprise and economic development.

Weber attempts to explain these correlations and raises the question of how types of economic activity deemed immoral and base at one time could be converted into a divine "calling" and an ornament of the spirit in another epoch. His answer is that social legitimization for capitalistic economic activity is to be found in the doctrines and dogmas of a number of nonconformist sects. Common to many of these is the notion of *personal responsibility* before God. In order to exercise this responsibility properly, life must be effectively and methodically *disciplined*. Each man is conscious that he is an instrument of God "called" to labor for His glory. Work, well and conscientiously performed, and success in business were signs that he was a member of the "elect," those who had been chosen by God for salvation. Thus an important result of ascetic Protestantism was a systematic ordering of the life as a whole and the creation of an army of disciplined workers to man the emerging productive and commercial machinery. The result was also to alter the value system of the middle ages and feudalism, and to produce a permissiveness and an *encouragement* of the systematic pursuit of economic gain in industrial and commercial enterprises. Furthermore, the worldly asceticism which Puritanism demanded impelled people to accumulate, discouraged consumption, and facilitated capital accumulation essential to economic growth.

In 1909, four years after *Die Protestantische Ethik* appeared, Felix Rachfahl[2] started a discussion of Weber's theories that has continued to this day in intellectual circles of Germany, England, Italy, the United States, and the Scandinavian countries. Werner Sombart, Lujo Bretano, William Ashley, R. H. Tawney, K. M. Robertson, W. Cunningham, A. Fanfani, J. B. Krous, T. S. Ashton, Wolmer Clemmensen, Talcott Parsons, Robert Merton and Wellman Warner[3] are among the many who have concerned themselves seriously with these theories. Many of these writers have criticized Weber on many points of this theory but usually concluded that the relationship between the Protestant Ethic and capitalism was plausible and valid even though many of them suggested alternative explanations of the relationship. One of the most frequent criticisms of Weber is that he ascribed the rise of capitalism to religion as a single cause. This accusation Weber anticipated and denied in these words: "We have no intention whatever of maintaining such a foolish and doctrinaire thesis as that the spirit of capitalism . . . could only have arisen as the result of certain effects of the Reformation, or even that capitalism as an economic system is a creation of the Reformation. . . . On the contrary, we only wish to ascertain whether and to what extent religious forces have taken part in the qualitative formation and the quantitative expansion of that spirit over the world."[4]

However, Weber's critics continued to belabor this point. Tawney, for example, thinks it unrealistic to hold that capitalistic enterprises could not appear until religious changes had produced a capitalistic spirit and he, like many others, ascribes the development of capitalism in Holland and England in the Sixteenth and Seventeenth Centuries as due to other economic movements particularly the Discoveries and other basic new economic developments,[5] and Bretano held that the influence of the Renaissance and Machiavelli was as great as Calvinism in breaking the bonds of earlier ethical restraints.[6] These points are also made by Kurt Samuelsson, a Swed-

[2] Rachfahl, F., in *Internationale Wochenscrift fur Wissenschaft, Kunst und Technik*, Nos. 39-43 (1909).

[3] For brief critical resumes of the ideas of many of these men see Kurt Samuelsson, *Ekonomi och Religion* (1957). Translated from the Swedish by E. Geoffrey French, *Religion and Economic Action* (Stockholm: Svenska Bokförlaget), 1961.

[4] Weber, Max, *op. cit.*, p. 75

[5] Tawney, Richard H., *Religion and the Rise of Capitalism* (London: John Murray, 1926), pp. 319, 320.

[6] Bretano, Lujo, *Die Anfänge des Modernen Kapitalismus* (München: K. B. Akademie der Wissenschaften, 1916), pp. 117-157.

ish economic historian, whose *Ekonomi och Religion* appeared in 1957. This book attacks Weber's theories all along the line and attempts to refute them, point by point. He concludes: "We can find no support for Weber's theories. Almost all the evidence contradicts them."[7] Samuelsson and Weber's other critics base their contentions on historical data from the same countries as Weber did, but they interpret the same data differently and choose different examples of Puritans or capitalists or documents to quote or cite to make their points. There is a tendency also to ignore materials which do not support the critical points they seek to establish. We are thus left with the problem of choosing between the logical deduction of proponents and opponents, and of determining the validity and relevance of one set of examples as against another.

The relative importance of various factors in the development of capitalism might be made clearer if we examine Weber's thesis in the light of data from different areas of culture, and materials from countries other than those considered by Weber and his critics, and events where historical developments have created a different sequence of events and whose different cultures and values have produced variations in motivational stimuli affecting religious belief and economic action. It would also be advantageous to consider results of some later research on this subject and bring to bear materials which have been left out through ignorance or design.

Robert Merton in "Puritanism, Pietism and Science"[8] traces the relationship between the Puritan Ethic and the development of scientific thought and science. His point is that the Puritan ethos exalted the faculty of reason; in his words: "Empiricism and rationalism were canonized, beatified, so to speak" and "thus made an empirically-founded science commendable rather than, as in the medieval period, reprehensible."[9] He points out that Puritan divines accepted a sensate standard of verification, and the idea of an underlying order in nature—two ideas essential to the scientific approach to the world. These ideas are supported by quotations from the writing and speeches of Puritans. The contention is further strengthened by his demonstration that the early scientists of the Seventeenth

---

[7] Samuelsson, Kurt, *op, cit.,* p. 154.
[8] Merton, Robert K., *Social Theory and Social Structure* (Glencoe, Illinois: The Free Press), 1949.
[9] *Ibid.,* p. 579.

Century, both in England and the continent, were overwhelmingly Protestant, and, furthermore, that Protestants encouraged and participated in scientific education to a much greater degree than did Catholics. Since technology is essentially the application of science to production and communication, the role of the Protestant Ethic in the development of science and the scientific outlook becomes relevant to economic development and a complement to Weber's thesis.

In "The Protestant Ethic and the Spirit of Capitalism in Norway"[10] I report the result of the application of Weber's thesis to a country whose economic and capitalistic development is different from that of Holland and England. This case is particularly fitting for this purpose since historical events and the sequence of events have eliminated some of the complicating factors present in other Protestant countries. In Norway, capitalistic enterprise and economic development as measured by economic indices did not show much development before some two generations after the establishment of a type of ascetic Protestantism. This sequence of events may, of course, be entirely fortuitous and not causally related, but when considered in conjunction with the nature of the expressed religious beliefs and values of the people and their recorded actions, the historical events and their sequential development suggest relationships which Weber's theories would lead us to expect. Early Lutheranism in Norway, because of its emphasis on grace, lacked, on the one hand, the sanctions for the most important result of ascetic Protestantism, a systematic, rational ordering of the moral life as a whole, and, on the other hand, the dogma that successful worldly work as a servant of God was necessary for salvation and a sign of a godly life.

Weber uses Benjamin Franklin as the example *par excellence* of a man governed by the Protestant ethic, but if he had known about Hans Nielsen Hauge, he would have found a man who by word and deed fitted his ideal type much better. Hauge and his followers started and operated economic enterprises all over Norway, often in places where none had existed before. By 1804, Hauge had organized widely ramified economic enterprises including farming, fish-

[10] Jonassen, Christen T., "The Protestant Ethic and the Spirit of Capitalism in Norway," *American Sociological Review,* 12 (December 1947), pp. 676-686.

ing stations, factories, mines, a paper mill and a foundry.[11] The Haugean revivals broke the cake of custom and the heavy crust of habit, and Haugeaners, peasants and farm laborers who had accepted their lot as inevitable and immutable, now gave up traditional ways and came to the towns to start businesses and factories and to take jobs as artisans. All of this was done with religious fervor and the conviction that to achieve eternal salvation one must be God's industrious and successful steward on earth. Thus the religious revivals of Hans Nielsen Hauge, which swept Norway in the early Nineteenth Century, transformed Norwegian Lutheranism into a religion that tended to produce the same behavioristic results as Calvinism had prompted in England, Holland, Switzerland, and France.

Weber's theories have also been tested in the study of the relationship between religious ideas and economic activity in nonwestern nations and nonprotestant countries. Robert E. Kennedy, Jr., in "The Protestant Ethic and the Parsis" (1962)[12] shows that the religious and ethical beliefs of the Parsis encourage the desire to accumulate rather than to consume goods, and the desire to maximize one's material prosperity as a sign of divine pleasure. This religion emphasizes the value of material work and accepts a sensate standard of verification and an underlying order in nature. Personal autonomy and individual responsibility are also strongly stressed. Kennedy then goes on to show that the Parsis are overrepresented in scientific, technical, commercial and industrial pursuits in India and how they, more than others, encourage and participate in scientific educational endeavors. The parallels between Parsis, Puritans, and Norwegian Haugianers are striking, and the relationships between the ideational content of these religions and the economic activity which is encouraged therewith appear to hold in each case.

A very interesting test of Weber's theory on a primitive society of Northwestern California has been made by Walter Goldschmidt

---

[11] A good account of the activities of Hauge and his followers as organizers and operators of business enterprises is to be found in: Dagfinn Breistein, *Hans Nielsen Hauge, "Kjbmand i Bergen,"* (Bergen: John Griegs Forlag, 1955). Hauge's religious and social ideas are described in his biography by A. Chr. Bang, *Hans Nielsen Hauge og Hans Samtid,* 4th Ed. (Kristiania: J. W. Coppelen, 1924); as well as in the large number of published works of Hauge among which are Werdens Daarlighed (1798), and *Loven og Evangelium* (1804).

[12] Kennedy, Robert E., Jr., "The Protestant Ethic and the Parsis," *The American Journal of Sociology,* 28 (July 1962), pp. 11-20.

(1951).[13] He traces the relationship between the "protestant"-like ethics of these people and their "capitalistic"-like economic structure and makes the following comparisons:

Northwest California and European Similarities

California	Protestant Europe
Socio-Economic Structure	
1. The hunting-gathering production	Industrial production
2. Traditional production techniques	Rational production techniques
3. *Private ownership of resources*	*Private ownership of resources*
4. *Money as a medium of exchange*	*Money as a medium of exchange*
5. Capital not profitable to owner	Interest as a source of power and wealth
6. No significant labor exploitation	Labor exploitation basic to economic organization
7. *Wealth status as a determinant of power*	*Wealth status as a determinant of power*
8. *Wealth as an indication of status*	*Wealth as an indication of status*
9. *Putative open class system*	*Putative open class system*
10. *Individuated family structure*	*Individuated family structure*
11. *Absence of fixed group orientation*	*Absence of fixed group orientation*
12. Small Homogeneous communities*	Increasingly urbanized communities
Ethico-Religious System	
1. *Individuated moral responsibility*	*Individuated moral responsibility*
2. *Work as a moral act*	*Work as a moral act*
3. *Asceticism in appetites, food and sex*	*Asceticism in appetites, food and sex* '
4. *The concepts of sin and guilt*	*The concepts of sin and guilt*
5. *Morality tales and personal preaching*	*Morality tales and personal preaching*
6. Supernatural beings and spirits	God as a stern Father
7. *Absence of priestly intercessor between man and supernatural*	*Absence of priestly intercessor between man and supernatural*
8. No concept of predestination manifest†	Concept of predestination

[13] Goldschmidt, Walter, "Ethics and the Structure of Society: An Ethnological Contribution to the Sociology of Knowledge," *American Anthropologist,* 53 (Oct.-Dec.), 1951.

* Kroeber notes (personal communication) the remarkably heterogeneous character of Yurok-Hupa towns compared to most primitive communities. It is for this reason he always refers to them as towns rather than villages. But culturally they would hardly seem as heterogeneous as the rising cities of the 16th and 17th centuries.

† But of this item Kroeber noted "I could make out a case for a sort of (predestination) too, though it wouldn't be quite Calvin's, and would take too long to develop here" (personal communication).

If we examine the above table it is clear that there are many similarities between the Northwestern Societies, Protestant Europe and Parsis India. The big differences, of course, are that these Californians are nonliterate and practice a hunting and gathering economy. Apparently a "protestant ethic" and a "spirit of capitalism" and capitalistic-like enterprise can develop without either Protestantism or Industrialism as long as the ethical system, whatever it is, gives social legitimization and encourages the morals, values and social relationships which are required for certain types of economic behavior.

That religion even today, when its influence is minimal in comparison to the Sixteenth and Seventeenth Centuries, is a vital part of American life and does influence everyday attitudes is well documented in Gerhard Lenski's *The Religious Factor: A Sociological Study of Religious Impact on Politics, Economics, and Family Life* (1961).[14] His findings in modern America that white Protestants rise further in the occupational world than do Catholics seem to reflect the observations of earlier writers using historical European data, and of Lenski's explanation of this phenomenon as being due to the Catholics' greater orientation to kin groups and less to values of personal autonomy, seems again to reveal the effect of a commitment to individual responsibility and action.

Calvinism, Haugeanism, and the ethical systems of the Parsis and the California tribes were essentially mental productions which achieved a psychological condition in men that produced particular behavior and habits which, in turn, facilitated the development of capitalism and an expanding economy.

There are probably many different idea systems that might produce a "spirit of capitalism"; that ascetic Protestantism did so for the Western world is Weber's great contribution to the sociology of knowledge, and to an understanding of the foundations of Western culture. Weber leaves open the question concerning the priority of spiritual as against material determinants of cultural trends when he states, "But it is, of course, not my aim to substitute for a one-sided materialistic and equally one-sided spiritualistic causal inter-

[14] Lenski, Gerhard, *The Religious Factors: A Sociological Study of Religious Impact on Politics, Economics and Family Life* (Garden City, New York: Doubleday & Co.), 1961.

pretation of culture and history. Each is equally . . ."[15] And Merton points out that the writings of Marx and Engels reveal a progressive definition (and delimitation) of the *extent* to which relations to production do determine knowledge and forms of thought.[16] It is probably safe to say that in a society the relationships between its ethical and economic systems are alternatingly reciprocal, at one period of time existential material conditions may affect the ethical system greatly, but at another time economic behavior may be decisively affected by a system of ethics which governs and integrates social life and rewards and legitimizes certain types of economic activity.

[15] Weber, Max, *op. cit.*, p. 183.
[16] Merton, Robert K., "The Sociology of Knowledge," Gurvitch and Moore, Ed., *Twentieth Century Sociology* (New York: The Philosophical Library) 1945, p. 374.

VII

THE THEISTIC BASES OF ETHICS

(This paper is a very brief summary of the main points in a lecture presented to a seminar on "Business and Ethics." The arguments are not worked out or presented in any detail. This is merely a sketch of a direction of thought and some of its conclusions.)

Marvin Fox

Problems of moral choice and decision are generated in part by the fact that there is no single pattern of approved action in human society. Cultural diversity is accompanied by moral diversity. Studies in cultural anthropology have taught us that there is almost no conceivable human act which is not somewhere approved and somewhere else condemned. The notion that the basic moral attitudes of our own society are universal is a bit of romantic (and perhaps ethnocentric) nonsense.

Faced with the fact of moral diversity, a man can not view his own moral attitudes as natural and, therefore, necessarily universal. His moral claims now require justification. Why is it wrong to murder, or to lie, or to steal? Why ought we be kind, generous, and honest? Most men, even those who are presumed to be virtuous, are not always *inclined* to satisfy the acknowledged demands of conventional morals. They do so in spite of their disinclination, and often at the cost of great personal discomfort. It is not always easy or pleasant to tell the truth. It sometimes requires inordinate self-restraint to keep from stealing, or inordinate self-discipline to be generous to an enemy. Why, then, should we feel bound to abide by moral rules which we find difficult or painful?

The most common answer is that it is expedient to abide by the rules, because if we do not we may suffer punishment. Official penalties, social ostracism, pangs of conscience, divine retribution—all these, and more, threaten the moral violator. But expediency is not a *moral* ground for moral behavior. This is easily seen if we consider the fact that most of us would insist on the binding character of a moral rule even if there were no punishment for violating it. No-

85

body wants to say that murder is wrong only because you probably can not get away with it, but that it is morally defensible if you do get away with it.

The appeal to expediency suffers from the defect which is common to every attempt to give an empirical foundation to moral principles. Empirical data only tell us what *is* the case, but every moral decision is concerned with what *ought* to be the case. Philosophers have long recognized that there is no way to move from factual to normative propositions. "Is" does not yield "ought." It may well be that one ought not do something, even though "everyone else does." We continue to insist that cheating on examinations is morally wrong, in spite of the claim of many students that "everyone does it." Similarly, the appeal to expediency, at best, tells us what the facts are, but gives us no *moral* guidance. The statement, "If you don't cheat you will fail the examination," does not have as its consequence, "Therefore, you ought (i.e., it is morally right) to cheat." This consequence only follows if, in my view, passing the examination takes moral precedence over honesty. But this, itself, is a moral decision and cannot be justified on any purely factual grounds. Preferences are not self-justifying, at least not from any moral perspective.

In the main tradition of Western philosophy we frequently find attempts to justify morals on rational grounds. Recognizing the insufficiency of empirical data, the appeal to reason seems to be the only alternative. From Plato to Kant, and beyond, philosophers have claimed to show that reason can give us the principles of morals just as it gives us the principles of mathematics. John Locke, for example, insisted that morals are mathematically demonstrable (though he never explained how).

Every purely rational moral philosophy encounters at least one insurmountable difficulty. This difficulty makes itself felt most when we attempt to go from general moral principles to particular moral decisions. Every student of Kant knows how hard it is to apply the categorical imperative to actual cases. So long as the categorical imperative is viewed as a principle of reason it seems to be purely formal, and for this very reason, incapable of guiding us in actual instances of moral perplexity. Reason, in its very nature, deals with the general, not with the particular. If mathematics and logic are thought of as the most characteristic products of reason, this is partly because they are the most general and abstract of all subject matters. But every moral situation is concrete and particular. It is concerned always with specific men in specific circumstances. Contemporary existential philosophy has shown us how incapable reason is of legislating the moral "ought." Whenever a philosopher moves from abstract general moral rules to particular cases, or even to the proposal of specific moral virtues he goes beyond the limits of what reason allows him.

Aristotle is an excellent example. Even if one agrees that the doctrine of the mean is a rational principle (and this is by no means obvious), the content of the mean depends on social convention. That courage is a virtue, and what its content is, can not be known by reason alone. Even less can we know by reason whether and how one ought to be courageous in given circumstances. Moreover, when Aristotle declares that some actions and passions are simply bad without qualification he seems to have gone far beyond reason. By what rational argument or principle can one show that adultery, theft, and murder are always evil? Is it a *rational* rule that "goodness or badness with regard to such things" do not "depend on committing adultery with the right woman, at the right time, and in the right way, but simply to do any of them is to go wrong?" (Nicomachean Ethics, 1107a15f.) However valuable reason may be in analyzing moral questions it can not supply us with the grounds of moral obligation.

It has been shown, as a matter of fact, that our very conception of duty is closely tied to the Biblical tradition. Western conceptions of right and wrong and good and evil, have their origin in our religion. The ethic of our culture was based initially on theistic revelation, and it is in that same theism that our morals have their deepest roots. The religious moralist offers no argument which he takes to be in itself sufficient to establish his claim. Beyond every argument is the act of faith in which he has committed himself to the moral values which he espouses.

In substance that act of faith affirms that our moral values are divine in origin and depend on a structure which is theistic. We cannot know that theft or adultery are evil simply by considering the acts or their consequences. Nor can we know that honesty and fidelity are good simply by considering the acts or their consequences. In every case we are appealing to a prior value commitment. Religious morality sees the source of that commitment as faith in the validity of the Biblical tradition. Without the divine source there is, from this point of view, no ground for making moral distinctions. We are seen as obligated because God has obligated us and, because of His creative act, has built special moral values into the very structure of being.

On what is this act of faith founded? For some it may rest on personal mystical experiences, for others on the claimed validity of the continuing teaching of a church, and for still others on arguments for God's existence and His moral nature. Each of these conventional types of defense can be shown to have serious defects. In the last analysis the belief in the theistic foundation of moral duty probably stems from the conviction that our very humanity is threatened without it. To be a person means, for us, to subscribe to the conceptions of moral value deprived from Biblical religion. The most fundamental of all Biblical value is human personality. Each man is taken to be absolutely valuable, and to have absolute dignity. It is for this reason that we recognize that we have moral duties to men, but not to animals or things. The dignity and worth of human personality derives in our tradition from the Biblical claim that man is a special creature formed in the image of God. If we deny this we reduce man to an animal and undermine the very foundations of morality. The faith that man has intrinsic worth is thus seen as depending on the belief in his divine origin. To deny this is to deny the meaning of our humanity and to reject the basis of all moral obligation.

VIII

ETHICS IN MANAGEMENT-CUSTOMER RELATIONS

W. Arthur Cullman

Before talking about the relationship between management of the firm and its customers, let us attempt to define Ethics. Other speakers have done this, but the definition I shall use today is that Ethics is the science of moral duty. This is a very simple definition. Actually, what we are looking for is how the concept of moral duty affects management-customer relations. If simplicity will aid understanding, then this simple concept may advance our understanding of the subject better than some more elaborate definitions.

In looking at business ethics, remember that a science involves careful analysis. It is necessary to classify what is meant by the various ethics that are applied to the relationship between the firm and its customers. Also, moral duty involves a subjective concept of *individuals*. *Firms* do not have ethics, but *people* in firms have ethics. Moreover, ethical concepts must be equally useful in both business and personal life. Many of the so-called ethical problems of business publicized recently are closely related to our behavior in educational institutions and in families. All of us are faced daily with ethical problems. A previous speaker pointed out that we are always seeking *to do right*. We must *feel* that what we do is right. Unless we feel right about what we do with respect to customers, we have no sound foundation for dealing with them.

Ethical standards have changed rapidly in recent years, largely as a result of the emergence of two basic ideologies. These have to do with the kinds of ethics we believe are effective. Ethics is, in part, an empirical consideration; what is and has been certainly affects what will be. For example, consider an old concept that the customer is dependent mostly upon his own efforts for getting value in an exchange. No one presumed that the function of business was to give or offer him values. It was the job of the customer to find and secure a value for himself. This sense of things has changed a great deal in recent decades, beginning, I believe, with the depression of the 1930's. In 1932, Franklin D. Roosevelt attempted to impose his own subjective set of values upon business. Not all of these were immediately accepted or converted into legislation, for there is a lag between development of social attitude and legislative enactment. Legislative action lags as much as a decade; however, administrative law, under which many ethical questions are decided, is more up-to-date. As a matter of fact, in some fields administrators are even *ahead* of general public and business thinking, as evidenced by the criticism by Newton Minow, Chairman of the Federal Communications Commission, that TV is a vast wasteland.

The second ideological aspect of ethics relates to what might be called uniformity within diversity. One may resort to the great philosophers or the great religious to find an ethical standard which will be applicable under all circumstances. It seems to me, however, that the ethics applicable to a specific situation must be pertinent to that situation, and it must express the ethical judgment of the individual making the decision. Aristotle stated this idea succinctly when he said: "Thought alone moves nothing." The ethics that you have are to no avail unless you operate with them and use them for actual decisions. He admonished one to find that which is most desirable; he indicated that virtue is more desirable than luck, that vice is worse than chance, that basic concepts are more important than their learned or environmental results. These to me are important ideas in ethics. They say to me that the generalities of religion and philosophy provide a common core of ethical appraisal, which is pretty much black or white, but that within cultural, religious, ethnic, or professional groups, the ethics of the individual, and the way in which he brings his values to bear upon a particular situation, is what really counts.

Let us apply this reasoning to the relations of business with consumers. It is what lies behind the attitude toward the customer that is important. Should a customer feel that he has received less value than he expected, that feeling does not set the ethical standard of sellers. The feeling of the individual who is making the sale decides the ethical quality of the transaction for the salesman. Every individual must have his own personal ethics to work from.

Consider, for instance, the personal feelings along this line which may be stimulated in transactions between a business firm and one of our largest customers—the United States government. Uncle Sam usually examines all sides of a question and requires competitive bids. An airplane manufacturer may use not only all the facts about his product but also what has become acceptable "Washington ethics," namely, entertainment of people influencing contract placement. Suppose that this firm receives the order. His competitor may feel that his product is just as valuable—meets all specifications —and his price was identical. Did they lose the business because they were afraid of being caught "influencing" government officials? Or did a personal code of ethics forbid the wining and dining of those officials? Has there, in this situation, been a breach of ethics? Is this unfair competition? Is this unethical competition?

Or consider a simpler analogous situation. Is it unethical for you to deal with a gas station that your brother-in-law works in because you know him? Is it unethical for you to go out of your way to purchase from someone who has done you a favor? This, in my opinion, is not unethical. I do not believe that it is unethical for the buyer for the government to purchase from the individual who has made himself pleasant. He has simply given extra service.

My personal code of ethics involves understanding what is presently acceptable in business practice. The values in the case of the government purchasing from the airplane manufacturer were identical. The decision was up to the purchaser who, in making it, considers everything that has a bearing upon the problem. The inference that because he was entertained he was influenced does not change my point of view one bit. Why not work with people that you enjoy, and since wining and dining are part of our business practice why not continue to use this in our business society?

Some firms have made quite a fetish of refusing to allow their salesmen to buy a lunch for a prospective customer. Some firms do not permit their purchasing agent to receive a lunch from anyone who is a prospective supplier. Because this appears to be humanly unacceptable, I do not feel that it has a chance of becoming ethically correct. We deal with friends. We talk to people face to face. We cannot possibly eliminate the normal amenities of human communication.

There is no question in my mind, however, that a substantial commercial bribe, something in the neighborhood of 5 to 10 per cent of the value of the contract involved is unethical. There is no magical percentage which can be applied, for the favor given must be considered in relation to the business to be placed, not only immediately but in the long run.

To be able to make such ethical decisions, one must develop standards of conduct and continue to evaluate them. We have to develop them individually, and in my estimation this is a process which begins very early in life. While it is timely for graduate students to consider these matters, it would be even better to have begun to think about them as an undergraduate, or even in high school and grade school.

I can perhaps illustrate some of the earlier influences upon my own present concepts of ethics by personal experience. When I was engaged in industry, before coming to teaching, I found that both our suppliers and our customers were often doing business the hard way. They were having difficulty producing minimal productivity on either side. With a little effort on my part, I found that I could help them be better businessmen and more successful. As they became more profitable from their own point of view, they also were better customers and suppliers for the company for which I was working—a cigarette manufacturer. That entranced me. Because of the shortage of skilled personnel during the war, this showed up more acutely than before. My own board of directors thought I was very clever because I was helping the firm secure needed goods and services. We were having trouble getting enough packaging, tobacco, machinery, and many other things. Because I was helping my suppliers do a better job, they took the extra productivity they were able to develop and allocated, or rationed, it to our firm. Any extra productivity they squeezed out of their plants they felt we deserved since we helped them. This posed an ethical problem to which I will return after presenting the other side of the situation—that of working with customers.

Our customers were scarcely customers in the true sense for we didn't have to sell them. Because of the shortage of cigarettes, they awaited us when our office opened in the morning and attempted to attract us with a variety of blandishments. They had all kinds of excuses and reasons why they (they were mostly wholesale tobacco distributors) should get an extra allocation—an allocation beyond what we had worked out on the basis of the share of our production which they had taken in the past. When these requests were made to me, I asked them to show me the distribution of their last order. Sometimes they said they didn't know where it went; sometimes they claimed that they took customers in the order in which they came in; others admitted that they sold where they could get the highest price. They rationalized this procedure on the ground that they had some "customers that bought at an inside price and they thought the right thing to do was to spread it to the small dealer," who, incidentally, paid the higher price. This bothered me a good deal, so I considered rationing additional supplies to any wholesaler who would furnish me with what I considered to be an equitable rationing system. When I had just gotten this worked out I had a visit from the OPA, who observed that a substantial portion of the company's production was going to dealers whose purchase price was higher than the average of all our sales in the past. This was when I began to wake up to some of the ethical implications of the entire problem. Was it fair that we should be distributing in this way? Was it unethical? Was it good customer relations? I was able to persuade the OPA that I had simply allocated those amounts which were already available and had not completely turned down any customer. They agreed that as long as a firm continued to sell some product at the prices which it was sold at before, there would be no complaint. The problem then seemed solved.

At that point, upon returning from a trip, I found that one of our management team had created another ethical problem. We had a retail store on Fifth Avenue, and he thought it would be nice to distribute the cigarettes through the retail store—one carton to a person. He had been allocating to our own retail outlet approximately quadruple what it had previously sold. This, of course, gave maximum distribution as each person got only one carton, and we controlled it completely. But our gross margin on over-the-counter retail sales was larger than our gross margin on sales through wholesalers. Was this ethical? Was it fair to customers? Was it fair to us? In my estimation, this was doing a perfectly ethical allocation job to the ultimate consumer, but it was unacceptable to our competition and customers. We were the only cigarette manufacturer with a retail store, and it was felt by some people that we should be prohibited from selling at retail any greater percentage of our production than we had before the shortage. After several conferences with government officials and trade association personnel, it was agreed that it was all right for us to sell up to double the percentage we had previously sold through our retail store. Where did that figure come from? What was the basis of it? Nothing, except that they wanted to have a mathematical concept that they felt they could explain at a later date. Was this ethics tinged with realism?

During his sale period a very large cigarette manufacturer persuaded our suppliers that, even though we had been so helpful to them and made it possible for them to be more productive, we should not get any larger percentage of output than we had prior to the shortage. It was suggested that compliance with this viewpoint would assure continued purchases after the war crisis was over. So we were squeezed from the suppliers' side. Now I am not trying to castigate this manufacturer for not having good ethics. He was merely fighting the war—a supply war—as best he knew how.

These experiences made me feel that somebody had to take a long look at how to run businesses with an ethical consistency that had not characterized the past. That was when I made up my mind that, if I could afford it, I would go into teaching. Two years later I worked out a plan which enabled me to do this, and now fifteen years later I am still at it.

To generalize from these experiences, I believe that a distinction, perhaps with a semantical overtone, must be made. Customers seem to want values, not facts. Our ethics persuade us to give them valuable facts—facts are often valuable to them. Still they do not care about the facts. When you buy something as an ultimate customer, you buy what you consider a good value. You part with your money for a combination of utilities or values. The ethical obligation toward the customer, therefore, is to give him the value that he wants. Manufacturers and middlemen, on the other hand, are distributing values, and values are judged by them and by their customers. In essence, then, my ethics stem from a belief in freedom of choice in its broadest sense. Any restrictions on freedom of choice by the consumer should be examined with care and subject to the democratic system for decision.

The question to which this leads is this: How does one derive his own value system so that he will not misrepresent values when working with customers? The problem is complicated by the fact that what you consider to be a value may or may not be considered so by the customer. You may make light of a transaction, saying that you "took" a customer by persuading him to buy something. If you told him the truth, if you did not in any way present him with a bit of information that was not factual, that is ethical, in my opinion. If you create a value for him by building an illusion around the product and he wants this value enough to pay for it, is there any reason why he should not be permitted to pay for it? It is perfectly ethical, in my opinion, to set a price to the ultimate consumer of $5 for perfume which may have cost only two cents to produce. And if a male may be persuaded that by dousing his female with this perfume he will get a very beautiful reaction, and therefore enjoy himself more, it may be worth $50 to him! I fail to see how we can say that a customer's values are being unethically handled when people who make the purchase receive what they want to receive for what they are willing to pay. This is a very simple concept but one which can be used in making decisions in many relationships with customers.

This raises another question: If happiness is the goal of human conduct, is personal profit happiness? This egotistic concept has been in philosophic disrepute for many years, and I agree with the philosophers who took it apart, because it doesn't solve the problem of making decisions. If you can secure happiness for yourself and the community, using the value concept in customer relations, you are broadening the scope and protecting yourself against the advent of the restrictive laws on one side and cultural pressures on the other side.

Some people view customer relationships altruistically, claiming that we should so serve customers that they receive the greatest good. To me this is highly illogical. Most discussions of altruism revert to utilitarianism. Too often one finds that when pressed concerning their altruistic motives people want others to be happy only if the others know who is the cause of their happiness. Further, they get personal, selfish satisfaction out of being told how happy they have made the other fellow. If you give your company or your goods away, you may think that you do it for altruistic reasons, but you more likely do it because you feel that you get a big reward.

How then do we decide what is good for the customer and the community, including ourselves? How do we decide what is and what is not ethical? I believe that this is a subjective process. It must be subjective, for ethics is the science of moral duty and science is developed from experience. It is from experience that we develop a sense of ethics which become our standard of conduct. My own ethics is based upon my business and professional experiences. Your ethics may be based upon different kinds of experiences. Communists have ethics. So do Gypsies. So do people who happen to be at odds with your or my personal sense of decency. They may not have our ethics, but they do have ethics.

It has been repeatedly brought out in these lectures that man is the ultimate value, that man's ability to get along is what we are searching for. We care less about things than we do about human beings; we care less about animals than we do about human beings. This is partially theistic, but also it is partially—and I think to a very considerable extent—the basis by which we make ethical decisions. We hurt ourselves when we do not recognize and choose the action that is ethical. Do we not know what is right or wrong from an inner sense that becomes more definite as we gain experience?

Sanctions are sometimes regarded as guideposts to making decisions, but we do not need sanctions, theoretically, if we consider happiness and perfection as the ultimate goal. Religious sanctions become dogmas. They are used by people who rely upon them even when they no longer make good ethical sense. Some religious concepts in the Judeo-Christian ethic are ludicrous in today's world. One of them is the idea of "turning the other cheek." When we are dealing here with an ideological concept, we cannot turn the other cheek—we have no cheeks left to turn! We have to face the frontal attack.

Social sanctions which operate through environmental factors have created some very peculiar things in the customer relations area, such as the complete acceptance of the practices of returning merchandise for full value to the store that sold it. Recognition of this practice carried to the extreme, became so general that a large store in Lincoln, Nebraska, put its label on the middle of the back of its evening clothes—outside to prevent customers from wearing clothes before returning them. Undeterred by this, high school students then made a fad of wearing the garments with the label so exposed. Is it ethical to return used merchandise? To what extent should this be sanctioned? The practice of adjustments is accepted as part of our way of living. Can a reasonable sanction be kept from being abused, and therefore can an ethical practice be kept from being unethical?

The concept of a legal basis of ethics might be illustrated in the sale of securities. Government authorities, acting in the interests of buyers, recognized the need for facts about securities. Therefore, regulations under the SEC were set up. Facts are now made available in the prospectus issued by companies. Yet despite the availability of facts intended to be protective, people bid up prices to seemingly unjustifiable height as soon as some securities hit the market. The SEC is investigating the rapid price rise. Is it the responsibility of the Securities Exchange Commissioners to prevent people, with facts available, from making purchases that they want to make? Is there an ethical obligation involved?

Similarly, if, through advertising, people are persuaded to discard useable products in preference for new, or to pay high prices for some publicized article, is an unethical act committed? This is a value judgment which, in my opinion, must be made by the customer. If he wants these things he should be free to buy them, as long as he is not injuring any portion of society. To prevent such things from being bought by people who are willing to pay for them would defeat a basic democratic ethic. It would place in the hands of a few people power to decide what is good for the entire population. Most critics of advertising, like most critics of the securities markets, want to be little dictators and to make decisions as to what is right and wrong for the other fellow.

When the interplay of subjective ethics between customer and firm continues, the variations between their ideas let ethical practice change at its own rate, and there is no enforcement of ethical standards set by one which may not be improved by others. We may move like the proverbial frog in the well which jumps two steps upward and slides one step back, but we move, and we move at our own rate. This, it seems to me, is exceedingly important.

IX

THE TRADE UNION MOVEMENT AND ETHICS

Alma Herbst

Strange as it may seem, the term "ethics" is seldom used in labor-management relationships. Nothing pertaining to this will be found in either the elementary or advanced textbooks on the subject; advanced research projects are not in this area. In fact, insofar as labor-management negotiations are concerned, ethics, as such, is not involved. That is not to say, however, that ethical standards do not govern the relations of management and labor in collective bargaining contract negotiation, in the grievance procedure, and in arbitration. Neither is it to indicate that ethics is involved in the labor union's management of its own affairs, or in the maintenance of standards of members. It is here within the trade union movement itself that lines of action can be found. As ethics in arbitration is the subject of the next paper, I shall confine my remarks to the ethical practices of the trade union.

The trade union movement in the United States and throughout the world is committed to democratic principles. It is a "must" with the trade union movement; it is its charter. In fact, it was often out of undemocratic circumstances that the union movement was organized and grew; it was a protest against aggression, domination, bad management, unemployment, and bad "conditions" from which relief or recognition was sought.

Unionism is the only institution through which the working people identify themselves as persons who are bringing about a democratic type of industrial economic organization to match the political. This cannot be achieved unless the movement is built upon ethical principles and practices of the highest order. Indeed the AFL-CIO has adopted a code of democratic practices as well as ethical codes to protect the rights and enumerate the responsibilities of members.

Today problems of democratic procedure and ethical practices become challenging areas because of the bigness of the unions, the bigness of the corporation, the bigness of the funds, the interdependence of the world. It is challenging and difficult because of the remoteness of the individual in the shop from his own union organization, and, in this respect, the trade union is little different from the university, the church, the business corporation. Each feels the pressures of conflict, tension, and crisis. The trade union movement has no monopoly on corruption or upon high ethical principles. There are two means of dealing with the situation: 1) the governmental, and 2) self-regulation.

I could intrigue you by talking about racketeering and corruption in the labor movement. We note that Mr. Jimmy Hoffa is again challenged. But how much of a rogue is he? Some people say that the Teamsters' Union should be readmitted to the AFL-CIO. What, after all, makes a racketeer? Is he made by a corrupt union, a million dollars, stock put in the names of wives, a court conviction? There have been all types of racketeering in the unions: robbery of union treasuries, bribery, extortion, use of hoodlums, depriving members of their insurance benefits. I took graduate work at the University of Chicago, where I knew about "Skinney" Madden and Al Capone, controlling in the 1930's perhaps two-thirds of the unions in the city of Chicago. With a combination of unscrupulous employers, labor shortages, highly competitive markets, migratory laborers, it was of advantage to the two groups for the boss and union leader to work in collusion.

I recall watching with Senator Paul Douglas a man whom we called "Umbrella Bill." He picketed the Memorial Chapel that was being built on the University grounds. As the building progressed, this man paraded around it. He carried an umbrella and a club, and the contractor or employer was supposed to toss a coin into the umbrella. "Throw a nickel on the drum and you will be saved!" Douglas said to me. "What can we do about this?" We knew that someday, depending upon how much nonunion labor was being used, or upon the adequacy of his bribe, a battering ram was going through one of the exquisite stained glass windows of that building. And we were not mistaken.

Before this, in the 1920's, the Lockwood Committee in New York began to unearth all types of corruption. For example, it is alleged that $180,000 had been collected from 19 of the city contractors before the culprit went to jail. It is interesting that such things occurred among groups not only of small contractors but among factory groups as well. How do you keep track of the wage earners working out of factories on construction, on trucks? In the late 1930's, there were numerous suits filed against building service employees convicted of extortion, of the theft of union funds, of evasion of federal income tax, and of collusion with employers. A peak was reached which was not pleasant to contemplate.

In the early days, the AFL was not vigilant in preventing or attempting to discipline unions in these matters. The major concern was the right to organize and recognition of the union. Moreover, on the one hand a convention resolution may be passed stating that everything must be aboveboard, that unions must be clean, that all wage earners are to obtain fair and equal treatment, that no discrimination shall exist, etc. At the same time the convention can reaffirm its position that every international union is autonomous. Bridging the gap between these two positions has been one of the very hard problems for the type of trade union federation in the United States, a federation of autonomous unions. The AFL-CIO is also built upon the principle of autonomy. However, as early as 1940, the presidents of international unions, including Walter Reuther, reported to the convention recognition of this problem. He and David Dubinsky of the International Ladies Garment Workers Union took the lead. The ILG President sought successfully to have the executive committee of the AFL-CIO expel international unions that refused to take action against dishonesty and collusion. The CIO as it came into being was accused of corruption and of communist infiltration. The report of the Civil Liberties Committee of about 15 years ago, states that there were a few union groups that were corrupt, that some were communist dominated, but by and large they were clean. In 1947 and 1948, during the presidency of Philip Murray of the CIO, there began the expulsion of dominated unions. An identification of ethical practices, bad practices, collusion-with-employer practices, and the communist-dominated groups was inevitable.

By 1951, the first resolutions were presented to the CIO convention on ethical practices. In 1952, a code on democratic rights was formulated; in 1953, a code on democratic rights and ethical principles. By 1954, Walter Reuther was told to establish a standing committee on ethical practices for the CIO. As you read the record, you find that the man who drew up that first code, and who continues to be interested in the subject, was Arthur Goldberg, who was then counsel for the CIO. He was named director for the Committee. The code dealt with powers to investigate malpractices in union administration and welfare funds. In 1955, at the time of the merger of the AFL and CIO, this beginning was extended and a standing committee established to consider ethical practices. It remains one of the leading committees, a five-member committee, of which President A. J. Hayes of the International Association of Machinists was and is the chairman. Two years later, 1957, the convention of the AFL-CIO adopted its Ethical Practices Code. There are now six Codes of Ethical Practices.

1. AFL-CIO Constitution
. . . On Ethical Practices
Article II, Section 10:

The objects and principles of this Federation are:

. . . To protect the labor movement from any and all corrupt influences and from the undermining efforts of communist agencies and all others who are opposed to the basic principles of our democracy and free and democratic unionism.

Article VIII, Section 7:

It is a basic principle of this Federation that it must be and remain free from any and all corrupt influences and from the undermining efforts of communist, fascist or other totalitarian agencies who are opposed to the basic principles of our democracy and of free and democratic trade unionism. The Executive Council, when requested to do so by the President or by any other member of the Executive Council, shall have the power to conduct an investigation, directly or through an appropriate standing or special committee appointed by the President, of any situation in which there is reason to believe that any affiliate is dominated, controlled or substantially influenced in the conduct of its affairs by any corrupt influence, or that the policies or activities of any affiliate are consistently directed toward the advocacy, support, advancement or achievement of the program or of the purposes of the Communist Party, any fascist organization or other totalitarian movement. Upon the completion of such an investigation, including a hearing if requested, the Executive Council shall have the authority to make recommendations or give directions to the affiliate involved and shall have the further authority, upon a two-thirds vote, to suspend any affiliate found guilty of a violation of this section. Any action of the Executive Council under this section may be appealed to the convention, provided, however, that such action shall be effective when taken and shall remain in full force and affect pending any appeal.

Article XIII, Section 1(d):

The Committee on Ethical Practices shall be vested with the duty and responsibility to assist the Executive Council in carrying out the constitutional determination of the Federation to keep the Federation free from any taint of corruption or communism, in accordance with the provisions of this constitution.

The Codes deal with a number of subjects: the issuance of local union charters; the administration of health and welfare funds; the problem of racketeers, crooks, communists, and fascists in the labor movement; the business interests or investments of union officials; the financial practices and proprietary activities of unions and union democratic processes. In 1958, the AFL-CIO Executive Council directed and required all affiliates to comply with the Code provisions.

The Ethical Practices Committee of the AFL-CIO has been instrumental in enforcing the Codes. As early as 1957, in its Convention Report it records its investigation of six international unions— of which three were expelled, two placed under monitorship, and one reinstated in good standing. The Committee continues to enforce the Codes and make recommendations at the request of the

Executive Council. Included in its work is the handling of complaints from individual union members against officers and officials.

For a number of years, trade union activities have come under Congressional investigation—by the Hoffman Committee, the Ives Committee, the Douglas Committee, the McClellan Committee. Doubtless because of disclosures made and the sensational handling of the hearings, the Labor-Management Reporting and Disclosure Act of 1959, popularly known as "Landrum-Griffin," was enacted in Congress. It should be noted that the trade union movement under the leadership of the AFL expelled the International Longshoremen's Association on grounds of corruption. This obviously preceded the findings and reports of the McClellan Committee. The AFL-CIO has not opposed legislation of a disclosure nature dealing with insurance, health, welfare, pension funds and other financial matters. It has reserved for itself the major responsibility of self-regulation to the end of establishing and maintaining a clean, free, democratic trade union movement.

Only today I had a letter from President A. J. Hayes: "As you are probably aware, the ethical practices committee conducted investigations into each of the situations disclosed by the McClelland Committee and on the basis of its findings (which were developed through investigations and formal hearings) it made certain specific recommendations to the Executive Council of the AFL-CIO. In every case these recommendations were adopted and the union involved was required—under penalty of suspension or expulsion—and expulsions and suspensions took place—to take directed affirmative action designed to eliminate wrongdoing which had been shown. Those that did not were expelled."

Several trade unions have established Public Review Boards to keep their organizations democratic and clean. The most noteworthy is that of the United Auto Workers; the Boards of the Upholsterers and Packing House Workers have scarcely functioned. The first public mention of the U.A.W. plan came in 1957 although it had been taking form for several years. An outside group of distinguished citizens was given responsibility to pass final judgment upon moral, ethical, democratic standards and procedures of the union. The final and binding decisions involve: 1) cases of individual members who feel they have been dealt with unfairly by their local unions or by the U.A.W. Executive Board (this includes local unions who have grievances against the international), 2) cases involving alleged violations of AFL-CIO Ethical Practices Codes.

A distinguished group of citizens has served as members of the U.A.W. Review Board—accepting Reuther's idea that "more and more the leadership of the labor movement must be prepared to have their stewardship . . . subject to public review." It is doubtless too soon to evaluate the impact of the voluntary impartial Review Board. Its creation evoked fears, hopes, sentiments; none of these have been fully established by the record as read either by labor's friends, enemies or leadership. On several occasions the Board Chairman has used the following statement:

> "I believe that I am voicing the conviction of my colleagues when I say that the creation of the Public Review Board reveals the high degree of stability, responsibility and moral health which American labor possesses and indicates that it has the capacity for self-discipline to enable it increasingly to remove the deficiencies and inequities from which no large organization is entirely free."

The trade union movement doubtless faces a crisis in many respects: decline in membership; difficulty of recognition and union security; inability to organize unorganized groups; the impact of automation and unemployment; the trend of governmental regulation of all aspects of collective bargaining as seen in the Labor-Management Reporting and Disclosure Act of 1959; the lack of unity within the trade union family and its lack of aggressive leadership; the need to establish sound and intelligent international contacts and programs; the impact of the union on the economy and responsibility for wage-price spiral. The list is incomplete. The trade union horizon has broadened to include security of income and job, participation in shop, community, and world affairs. It encompasses the recognition of the individual and his place in an ever-widening group. Problems of democracy and of ethical practices assume a position of ever increasing importance within the trade union. These emerge within the union family, in the consideration of each of the contract provisions (seniority, grievance handling, wages, pensions, etc.), in the elimination of graft, corruption and dishonesty.

As George Meany, President of the AFL-CIO, has stated:

"The AFL-CIO is committed by word and deed, to the concept that free, democratic trade unionism must be clean, honest trade unionism."

X

ETHICS IN MANAGEMENT-LABOR RELATIONS: ARBITRATION

Glenn W. Miller

I shall use the term "ethics" to mean "due regard for other people." In the relationships with which labor arbitration is concerned, it is much the same thing as that which is "customary or traditional." Often in grievance work one is concerned with activities which fail to meet someone's concept of what has been past practice, custom, or tradition. Thus, it may be said that concern for ethics in management-labor relations is a concern in the relations of management and labor for the rights of the other party.

While there are exceptions to the generalization that ethics are not involved in the *bargaining* relations between management and labor, it is generally true that negotiation of agreements is a power relationship. Equally important in labor relations, however, is the application of the agreement reached between labor and management—the breathing of life into the agreement. Even if agreements are negotiated largely out of power and capacity to negotiate, the *interpretation* of the agreements from day to day involves not power but ethics.

For example, a section of an agreement on promotion may say that the senior person shall be promoted if his capacities are reasonably equal to those of someone else. When you get to an issue of whether or not one man or another should be promoted—one being junior but allegedly having more ability or better physical fitness, then the need arises to determine what the agreement means—what is the meaning, in a judicial atmosphere, of the agreement negotiated out of a power relationship. Here there is a considerable element of the ethical involved.

The very genesis of the trade union movement, in fact, grew out of the real or fancied absence of ethical behavior on the part of management. Why else would union organizations have developed, to try to build the power of workers, except that they felt that they were not being treated fairly and had to have some kind of a power block with which to defend their position or to induce more acceptable behavior? One might say that they developed to build their power so that they could extort concessions from the other party. This, I think, is far fetched and does not explain the struggles and the difficulties involved in the building of the union movement. It was a groping for adequate power to induce management to behave with a reasonable regard for the rights of the persons who work for them. Perhaps it can be said that the union movement is a countervailing force to the improper exercise of power.

When one gets into the day-to-day relationships between labor and management—and this occupies three-fourths or more of the time of regular local union officers in the country—most of the union activities pertain to what the members consider to be unfair or unethical. A grievance builds up for some reason; a worker or group of workers, or the officers of the union, feel that someone is treated unfairly. They then try to relate this to a particular provision of the contract. It will then be dealt with under the grievance procedure. Many things come up in an agreement which never gets to the grievance stage, about which no one feels very strongly that there is any improper or unfair behavior involved. One thing that gives rise to much trouble, either in negotiation or in grievances, is the fact that both parties (and there may be a third party, namely, the public), although behaving as sincerely as they know how, may have sharp differences in their positions because of their orientation. The orientation of management is that they ought, in their labor relations, keep as much freedom of decision making and freedom of operations, as possible. It is an individualism-oriented philosophy. The basic attitude of the worker or unionist is quite different. It is a security-orientation. To the worker, security may mean security on the job, security in old age, or other aspects of economic security. There is a vast difference between these two orientations.

The significance of this is the fact that the labor-management relationship is a *conflict relationship*. The conflict has to be recon-

ciled, adjusted, or compromised—so that the parties can work together. Basically, nevertheless, a compromise relationship is involved.

One way to show this conflict that comes up in labor relationships is to look at several cases in which I have acted as arbitrator,
to suggest some of the types of problems and ethical issues that are
involved. Keep in mind that this does not concern negotiation nor
the internal affairs of the union. Keep in mind also that when you
have a trade union agreement—and there are some 100,000 of them
in the country today, covering perhaps 18,000,000 workers—this
whole document is essentially a set of statements of rights and duties.
Every right carries with it a correlative duty. This is what comes
up in individual cases, where it seems that a right has not been
observed. In other words, another party did not perform its duty,
or respect the right of an individual.

A few years ago, a man was working in a type of job that was
quite seasonal. He and everyone else in the place of work—every
member of that local—were laid off for part of the year. Most of the
year they had pretty good work, but for three or four months they
were laid off. It was important that in the agreement there be a
well worked out procedure for lay off and recall. Both were based
upon seniority, with the provision that recall notification would
be sent by registered letter to the worker's address, and that he had
five working days in which to report back to work. In this case, the
man laid off during the slack period got a job with a construction
company earning more money than he made on his regular job.
He received a notice to return to work. Looking at the calendar, he
saw that he could work on the construction project until the end
of a pay period and still return to the company on the fifth working
day, the last day of the "grace period" allowed in the agreement.
He gave a notice that he was quitting work, but he did not give a
notice to his regular employer that he was coming back. On the day
of his return, unexpectedly a wildcat strike was in progress at the
plant. Being a union man of some years, he did not want to cross
the picket line so he returned home. The strike lasted two or three
days. On the day that the plant did open, when he returned to work,
arriving 15 minutes before the shift opened, he was told that he

had no job because he did not report back in five working days. A grievance was filed asserting that the three days of a wildcat strike, when no work was done in the plant, were not properly to be considered as part of the five work days specified for returning to work. Whether they were or were not, does one want to be a stickler for the letter of a contract? There are surely some ethical overtones here. Here was a man of several years' service with the company who was able to prove that he was at the plant before work was to start on the fifth work day following his recall. He did report to work on the fifth actual day of work after his notice. While I think there is an ethical issue involved, I suspect that you could decide this case on the basis of the contract alone. The issue, however, in the mind of the union representative who filed this case was that this man had been treated unfairly.

Another case: A senior worker in a small department of a large plant, a woman with 16 years seniority on the job, was laid off and a much junior person was kept on the job. The reason was because the contract said that seniority should govern in layoffs if the ability of physical fitness was relatively equal. The company said that the woman was laid off because, had she stayed on the job she would have had to handle weights occcasionally in excess of 35 pounds. While no state law prohibited this in the state in which the case arose, it had been the custom not to put a woman on a job where she had to lift more than 35 pounds. In the hearing, a company man indicated that one part of the job that she performed was to empty containers by a hand process, and it was estimated that the two vessels she carried sometime weighed 40 pounds or more. This had been going on for years. Management had not worried about this before! Here again an ethical overtone is involved. If you feel that the woman was treated unfairly, you then look at the contract to see how you can justify a grievance.

A third example was a case of a breakdown in a piece of equipment, a track along which heavy equipment rode. The equipment included a rail somewhat like a railroad track. In general, on Sunday no repairmen were kept on the job, although at this particular time, on Sunday, three repairmen were in the plant working on another job. The company assigned these three people, who were already at the plant, and called in one track repairman to do the repair work, asserting that the repair had to be made promptly because heavy machinery would have to traverse this section of track within a few hours. The union then filed a grievance, asserting that the company should have called three other men (track repairmen, the union insisted) out on overtime and kept the three repairmen already there on the work they were doing prior to the breakdown. They claimed that the company had no authority to assign these men already at the plant to this particular kind of work. Here you have an example of what I would call an unfair point of view on the part of the union. I felt it was an attempt to take advantage of an emergency situation to pick up overtime for other persons in the local. It was not a very reasonable way of trying to conduct a relationship where there was some element of emergency.

Still another case: A couple of boys were told to come in on a Saturday in a small plant. They assumed that they would work in their own home department and were not told otherwise, but they were taken to a different department where a foreman put them on a particular job quite unlike the work they normally did. Soon the foreman decided that they really could not do this job, and he asked one of them to go on a different kind of work. He kept the other on this job and brought in a man from his own department to work with him. The man, shifted to the other type of work and away from his buddy, did not want to do it, and the foreman simply answered: "Either do it or go home." He went home. The company suspended him for three days for refusing an order. The man said that he did not refuse the order; he said he had an alternative given him, "Do the job or go home," and he took his choice. Again there was a certain ethical element involved, when a man was disciplined for less than adequate communication by the foreman.

A final example is a small plant of less than 100 people working under its first contract. Relationships had not shaken down. The president of the local union (young—only 21—not too well educated) had been instrumental in preventing workers from moving from a company union setup to a local union of an international organization. Sometime during the year, a grievance occurred which was not settled but hung on. At the beginning of the second shift (which was small—not over 25 workers), there was a conference held again to discuss this grievance. The president of the local worked on the second shift. When he came downstairs at the end of an hour and a half of fruitless bickering over this grievance, for no reason except that it was known that no agreement had been reached, the workers stopped their work. The local union president, who had never handled such a situation, left the plant without ringing out to go to the staff representative who had serviced this local, and who had an office a couple of blocks away. He returned half an hour later, and the company fired him for being away from the job without ringing out; they admitted later that they did it to discipline their employees for improper behavior. Because the president of the local, more than anyone else, bears responsibility, he was fired. Here again a question of ethics is involved. In this case, I ruled that the man should have gone back to work. Then I received a 50-page memorandum from the lawyer presenting the company's case, asking for reconsideration. This I did not do. To me it involved action with due regard for another person who was also a human being. Undoubtedly, he should have rung out or at least told someone that he was going out for help. He did not do these things, but I believe he was trying earnestly to discharge certain responsibilities that rested on him.

There is another facet of ethical relationships that has not been touched upon. We are getting now an increasing amount of government intervention in labor-manager relationships. The recent incident in the steel industry illustrates what I have in mind. It has been a growing development for a couple of decades, certainly since World War II. Although the major steel strike in the Eisenhower administration was settled through government pressures, the pressure in this instance was indirect. We are getting the implication in central governmental intervention that the actions of labor and management may not be conducive to the best interests of the public as a whole. Put differently, using the basis of social welfare, they are unfair, unjust. I gather that the pressures in Washington now are a rather significant extension of central government powers, primarily presidential powers, to intervene in labor-management relationships. The threat is very real, very major, and it is quite likely that the present legislation, which amounts to one section of Taft-Hartley, plus railway labor legislation (which applies also to airlines), plus whatever pressures the President can apply, will be expanded. There is pressure for extension of these powers into a sort of "kit of tools" that may allow a half dozen different approaches that might be used, at the discretion of the President. The assumption seems to be that if people do not know what alternative may be used they can not quite assay the pressure on them contrasted with the other party, they may bargain more seriously and more earnestly.

There is a certain mount of fear involved in this growth of increasing central pressure over labor relations. On the other hand, I am not sure we can get by without extension of the central government power, because as unions in general have tended to grow more powerful, as companies have gotten larger, and as industry-wide bargaining has taken on more frequency, there are more instances when the nation may be hurt by the failure of the parties to reach a satisfactory settlement. On the other hand, the public many times may fail to see exactly the thing to which they are reacting. Many times the public seems to want intervention when actually there is only public inconvenience, not public hardship. It is easy to confuse the two. I suggest, for example, that there was no need of presidential intervention via Secretary Goldberg in the recent steel dispute. The steel dispute had almost four months to run before the steel contract expired. Why the great anxiety to get a settlement? Of course, much stockpiling would have occurred if a settlement had not been reached before the last minute prior to the expiration date, and major cutbacks probably would have followed the settlement. There would have been major economic repercussions. Even so, were we as a nation faced with a sufficient *emergency* to warrant such intervention in "Free" collective bargaining?

Not unimportant, when you are dealing with the question of rewriting the allowable area of labor-management relationships (to hedge it about much more, often to protect the public against inconvenience rather than major hardship), I question sincerely whether this is wise or not. But the issue will not be discussed on the basis of wisdom; it will be discussed on a quasi-ethical principle of protecting the public against hardship. You may call this public ethics, if you will.

XI

ETHICS IN BUSINESS-COMPETITION RELATIONS

Theodore N. Beckman

This is a very difficult subject on which to prepare, so any of the things which I am going to say will be said in a rather informal manner. Sort of thinking aloud. It does not mean I have not been preparing, but the preparation is more in the nature of an outline of a sequential arrangement in which to present a relatively few thoughts and ideas I have on this subject.

In considering this subject, let us first deal with the meaning of "ethics." To observe what authorities have said about ethics in general, and ethics in business in particular, I have examined three sources. Webster's Third *International Dictionary*, in substance, defines ethics as the discipline dealing with what is good or bad, right and wrong, with moral duty and obligation. Note that ethics is basically defined as a discipline dealing with what is good and bad, right and wrong. Of the several subsidiary definitions, one is that ethics is a group of moral principles or set of values. Instead of a discipline or a study, it is an aggregation of moral principles. Also, ethics consists of the principles of conduct governing an individual or profession. In a second source, *The Columbia Encyclopedia*, was another interesting statement. Ethics is looked at there as it is viewed in philosophy, and reference is made to it as a study of evaluation of human conduct in the light of moral principles. These moral principles can be viewed either as the standard of conduct which the individual has constructed for himself, or a standard of conduct, a formal set of values, which has been imposed from the outside. Here philosophers differ, depending upon whether the philosopher is an institutionist, an empiricist, an idealist, an egotist, a hedonist, or what have you. In still another source, a good ordinary dictionary of contemporary American usage, by Bergen Evans and Camelia Evans, was another interesting succinct statement. Ethics and morals, once upon a time, were synonymous—ethics was a Greek word, morals was Latin. Now, in common usage, distinction is made between the two. The distinction indicated is that ethics is the science of morals, and morals are the practice of ethics. That is how they are related.

Reasoning from these authoritative statements, the matter may be summed up as follows:

1. The Concepts of Ethics—Ethics is conceived to be a discipline, a science, a study, an evaluation. It certainly belongs in the field of education. However you regard it, it is a study.

2. Content or Subject Matter—The content or subject matter of ethics is what is good and bad, right and wrong. You frequently encounter, in connection with that subject, terms like truth, fairness, justice, which would seem to indicate that the things that are true, fair, and just are ethical; conversely, that which is untrue, unfair, and unjust is unethical. To know what is true, fair, and just requires judgment, which brings me to the third point.

3. Judgment—Judgment must always be used in terms of human conduct. We differ in this regard from the psychiatrist who searches for real motives behind the behavior. In our motivational research we are simply judging the outward behavior, the overt act, and not so much the propelling force behind it. Behavior is what is emphasized and not the cause of it. We are studying the behavior to determine whether it is true, fair, just. In other words, whether it is right or wrong, good or bad.

4. Standards—There is a prerequisite for that judgment, namely, a set of values. One has to have a standard by which he can judge. Conduct cannot be judged without a standard.

5. Values—Standards must be in terms of a set of values, which may be personal. The more personal the better, because that which is within us probably lasts longer and means more to us. However, values are often not personal or individual but those imposed by society. "Society" might be a profession, a trade association, the government, or even the sampler of social mores. We do not do certain things because society would frown upon them. The important point is that there has to be a set of values, either personal or from the outside; very often it is a combination of both.

Historically, ethical conduct in business has been at a much lower level than in other areas of human conduct in everyday living. Thus, while *The Book of Common Prayer* includes the injunction to do to all men as you would they should do unto you, in Charles Dickens' writings you will find the following rule for bargains: "Do other men, for they would do you." This is followed by the questionable statement, even for his times: "That is the true business precept."

To be sure, there are still many persons in business who do things in the conduct of their business affairs that they would not think of doing in other areas of their living. This is done under the pretext that "business is business," as if business were entirely divorced from ethical considerations. Other justifications or rationalizations for doing the unethical in the conduct of business are: all other businessmen are doing the same thing, or that it is essential for survival or for progress in these days of tough competition. Thus, it is unfortunate that at this time there are still many businessmen, usually small ones, and occasionally some real big ones, who follow the Dickens precept.

To recapitulate, the point I want to emphasize is that ethics in business is more comprehensive than what is covered by laws or regulations which are prepared for the guidance of administrative agencies, and by court interpretations. Let me give you an example of actions that are not required by law or by regulations or by courts: the return-of-goods privilege. One store here in town frequently accepts goods returned by customers which were never bought at that store—they go even that far on the assumption that the customer is always right. Similarly, credit is based on confidence and on many things which are not required by law, regulation, or judicial decision. In our daily conduct in business we do many things merely because they are considered ethical but not required by law. Ethics is a more comprehensive term than what we call legality or lawfulness.

Nevertheless, the legal framework in which business operates, in my judgment, provides the most substantial basis for ethical conduct in business. That being the case, for a proper appreciation of this legal framework, especially on the national level, we must go to the basic philosophy which underlies antitrust policy and the whole relationship between the federal government and business. Many of the states have followed the federal government along the same general lines. You will find that there are two major or principal objectives in that philosophy. One of them is to preserve and promote competition. Professor Fulda of our Law School, speaking at this seminar, indicated a number of important ethical connotations and implications of this. He discussed the freedom of opportunity which competition provides, the protection against abuse that comes from a concentration of power, the reward for superior performance, and an incentive to work in the public interest. All of these were pointed out by him as implications and connotations of that first objective in our antitrust policy, namely, to preserve and promote competition, because from competition we get these and other benefits.

However, it is not enough to have competition, hence I want to dwell on the second big objective: to prevent or minimize unfairness in competition. This is altogether an ethical question. Being fair or unfair, just or unjust, true or untrue—all of this is embraced in that second phase of basic philosophy. I want to emphasize this particularly, Section Five of the F.T.C. Act which gives the Federal Trade Commission authority to determine what is unfair. Let us consider some of the guides which the Federal Trade Commission has consciously or unconsciously used to determine whether a certain competitive practice is unfair. In this it has been guided, it seems to me, by several criteria. One is whether the practice, act, or method is against good morals. For example, fraud, deception, and misrepresentation would be regarded as against good morals. Even the ordinary man with any conscience would admit that that is not the way to conduct ourselves. A whole host of business practices have from time to time been prohibited on the ground that they are against good morals. That, by the way, changes from time to time; the number of practices so prohibited is constantly increasing. Now, is this because business is getting worse or is it because our standards are getting better? I am inclined to think the second is the reason, because the Federal Trade Commission and the courts which have supported it in various appeal cases have constantly attempted to raise these standards of ethics. They now outlaw many practices which heretofore were not deemed unfair. Often I am told by a businessman: "I have been doing this for thirty years and nobody raised any questions; now all at once they tell me I can not do it." That businessman is just as ethical today as he has been for the last thirty years. He is not worse. He may be better. But the thing that he has been doing for thirty years he can not do now because the Commission, after careful investigation of similar cases, has decided that it is unfair. When, because of the large and growing number of practices which have been prohibited, it is claimed that business is going to the dogs, I think just the opposite conclusion should be drawn.

A second kind of condemned practices and methods are those which are trade restraining and monopolistic in nature. In such cases, the Federal Trade Commission, under Section V, may be interpreting violations of other laws: the Clayton Act or the Sherman Act, for example.

At this point, let me digress for a moment. The two main objectives of our philosophy in relationship of government and business are implemented by what we call antitrust policy—antitrust policy on the federal level. On the state level we have many duplications to cover commerce within the states. Speaking only for the time being of the federal level, this policy is implemented basically by three fundamental laws and their amendments: (1) The Sherman Act and amendments to it, the most important amendment being the Miller-Tydings Act which excepts fair trade from the Sherman Act prohibitions; (2) the Clayton Act with two important amendments, one of them, passed in 1936, known as the Robinson-Patman Act, and another amendment, passed in 1950, the Anti-Merger Act, which is an amendment to Section Seven of the old Clayton Act; (3) the Federal Trade Commission Act, also passed in 1914, and amendments to that, like the Wheeler-Lea Act and some others. There are many other acts which are enforced by the Federal Trade Commission, but these three are basic.

Now, let us get back to consider the things which guide the Federal Trade Commission. One of its responsibilities is to eliminate unfairness. The second one is to prevent all of those acts, practices and competitive methods which are monopolistic or trade restraining in a substantial way. A third set has to do with discriminating practices. They are covered primarily by the Robinson-Patman Act, which deals with discrimination between the different customers which may affect competition substantially through that discrimination. Finally, it is concerned with self-destructive acts which in themselves seem to be perfectly justified; carried too far may destroy the very thing that makes them possible. This can be illustrated by the practice of selling below cost. If that selling below cost is of a predatory character (not because you are more efficient, lowering the price because you do a better job, and in that case you can stay in business indefinitely, society benefitting from it), if you have cut the price below your cost and you are actually losing money, the only conclusion that can be reached is that you are doing it for a predatory purpose, to drive somebody else out of business. If you are successful in doing that, then what will happen to those prices? In the long run, those prices are going to be higher because it will destroy the very thing which makes this price cutting possible. Now, I could elaborate on that a great deal, but I am not going to do it, because there is a lot of material to cover within the limited time at my disposal. While there are a number of things with which I have to deal, I want to give you an illustration of local price cutting covered by point number four used for guidance by the Federal Trade Commission in determining what is unfair competition. I have reference to the Anheuser-Busch case with which you were asked to get acquainted. It also points out the difficulty of doing what my colleague (Professor Bartels) wanted me to do and that is to stick to the topic which he assigned to me, which is practically impossible. In other words, you can not say that you are going to discuss ethics in management-competitor relations and disregard its other relationships including relationships with customers because they are all intertwined. Now, let us take for our example the Anheuser-Busch case, involving the people who make Budweiser beer. That company cut the price in the St. Louis market in order to meet the lower price of competitors. The company was losing business in that market very heavily. Its beer was selling at a premium considerably above the other brands. Then it decided that it could not continue to do this, so it cut the price, but it did not reduce the price on its product in other areas—only in St. Louis. So, the Federal Trade Commission brought action against a company on the grounds that its price cutting, local price cutting, was discriminatory in character. It affected, it claimed, three kinds of competition. Remember that there are three levels of competition with which the Robinson-Patman Act deals as well as some of the other acts. One is the seller's competition. It is competition with the seller's competitors. I am supposed to stick to that. Competition among competitors. We call that primary-line competition. Here it was found that the competitive sellers were not affected by the reduction in price of Budweiser. From the facts it was discovered that some of the competitors were growing, taking a bigger share of the market, and some of the competitors were losing out but for other specific and identified reasons. Hence, the primary-line competition was not affected. Then there is buyers' competition designated as secondary line. The question here was whether the customers to whom Budweiser was sold were discriminated against. The findings did not justify such a conclusion because all of them were charged the same price exactly, so we had no disturbance (i.e., no discrimination on the secondary line). Then we go down to the customers' customers. In other words, the buyers' customers' competition and that is tertiary-line competition.

The question which has come up, for example, in this case is the same which I mentioned in the assignment having to do with the Federal Trade Commission's action against Sylvania and Philco which involved a discrimination in price in which Sylvania was selling to Philco at a price about 15¢ per radio and TV tube lower than what Sylvania was selling to its distributors. Of course, the Sylvania distributors were selling the replacement tubes to Sylvania's retailers or dealers. Philco was selling its tubes to Philco distributors and Philco distributors were selling them to Philco retailers who were mainly appliance retailers. The point was that the lower price received by Philco could be passed on and it was claimed that it was passed on to the Philco distributors so that these buyers from Philco were competing unfairly, presumably, with the distributors who bought the same tubes directly from Sylvania. You see, it was not a question of competitors on the primary level because Sylvania charged exactly the same price to all other manufacturers of radio and TV equipment. In other words, any manufacturer who would have wanted to buy those tubes would have had to pay the same price and would have received the same concession that Philco did. But it was on the secondary line that competition was supposed to have been affected unfavorably, and also on the third line. This illustrates my point that you cannot possibly separate the effect of a price discrimination on one level from the effect on other levels. They all intertwine.

Now, coming back to the Anheuser-Busch case. Here it was argued by the Commission that by cutting the price in St. Louis and not elsewhere the company was discriminating geographically. The case was finally decided late in 1961 in favor of the company.

What were some of the ethical questions involved? One was the question of good faith. Isn't that an ethical or moral question —good faith? Did the company cut the price to meet the competition or others *in good faith*, which means on the basis of real honest-to-goodness knowledge as to the prices the others were selling at and was merely trying to *meet* such competition? Another criterion that was used in the case was whether there was a vindictive motive in the price cutting. Did the company have vindictive motives in cutting that price by trying to put something over on somebody? The matter of punitive effects was another criterion used. Not only the motivation was considered, but also the effects. Were the effects punitive? Did the company try to punish competitors? Lethal weapons was another term used by the courts. Ordinary weapons were fine, but were there lethal weapons used that would tend to drive the competitors out of business? Another term used was that of misused economic power or size. Misuse. You can use your economic power, which is exactly what the Robinson-Patman Act permits you to do. You can buy cheaper than others do (i.e., than your competitors), provided it can be justified on economic grounds, or by meeting competition in good faith.

The Standard Oil Company of Indiana case is a good example of meeting competition in good faith. It took 17 years for that case to be straightened out. The company found it important enough to fight it out and the case went to the Supreme Court twice, to the Circuit Court of Appeals twice, and to the Federal Trade Commission twice. Since it was a first case along that line, it took a great deal of time before it was finally decided whether Standard Oil of Indiana was selling its gasoline to certain customers in Detroit at lower prices in order to meet competition in good faith, and whether there was good faith. That in itself had to go up to the Supreme Court once, just for that point alone.

So you see, in the Anheuser-Busch case, practically the whole thing was a question of ethical conduct even though it is basically covered by law. If the company had done the same thing that it did, vindictively, punitively, with punitive effects, in bad faith (notice that we talk about good and bad faith), using weapons that are recognized as lethal(as bad as carrying a gun when you have no license to do it), misusing its economic power, if it had lost money in the St. Louis market as a result of the price reduction and made up for it by charging higher prices elsewhere, then the Anheuser-Busch Company would have lost the case. Here is a good example of how many ethical considerations can be involved in determining whether a thing is done lawfully or not.

Now, my thesis is that the present legal framework, and such framework as is constantly evolving, provides the basis for a rather high standard of ethical conduct in business. Remember that when you are dealing with the legal framework you are concerned not only with the original laws as passed or as amended. That is only the beginning. When a law is passed, it is handed over to some administrative agency for enforcement and that agency immediately proceeds to study the law, the Congressional Record, the various committee reports of the Senate and the House, in order to see what the real thinking was behind the passage of that law. And then what does it do? It then proceeds to develop rules and regulations for the guidance of the administrative staff in enforcing that law. So, first, you have to know the law itself. Then you have to know what all of these administrative interpretations are, what these guides are. Just recently the Federal Trade Commission had decided to do a lot of that sort of thing. I have here "Guides Against Deceptive Pricing," issued by the Federal Trade Commission. Here I also have "Guide for Advertising Allowances and Other Merchandise Payments." These were formulated in order to give the Commissioner's interpretation. They are not final. They are not enforceable *per se*, but they are guides indicating what the Commissioners are thinking, as an enforcing agency, as to the meaning of these matters covered. Then there is a third area which deals with court interpretations and decisions. This is going on all of the time. That is why you have to keep up with court decisions and interpretations constantly. When you get this legal framework, consisting of those three things, the laws themselves, the rules and regulations governing them as brought out by the administrating agency, and the various court decisions which are constantly coming into the picture, only then do you get a proper understanding of the appropriate laws and their practical application. My point here is that *the present legal framework which is constantly evolving furnishes the means and guidance for very high ethical standards of business conduct.*

To illustrate further how the legal framework is constantly evolving and how much of ethics is involved in the various actions taken on the legal front, I have brought with me weekly reports from one of the Trade Regulation Services for the last several weeks. These are in the form of summaries followed by the detailed material that is rather comprehensive and voluminous. For our purposes, let me just refer to the May 7th weekly summary. Here I marked one item in which the Carter Products, Inc., was prohibited from using commercials on TV which *falsely* disparaged competing products. You know this is the company that makes "Rise" shaving cream and in the commercials it compared its shaving cream with what it called *ordinary* shaving cream and it demonstrated that ordinary shaving cream dried out quickly before you had a chance to shave, but its products stayed moist and did the job. Upon investigation, it was found that the ordinary shaving cream which the company used in its commercials for comparison purposes was not shaving cream at all. It was some kind of a concoction that was made of something that does dry out but it had nothing to do with the ordinary shaving cream. So it was disparaging the competing products and playing up its own. It was ruled to be an unfair competitive practice and accordingly the company was ordered to cease and desist from using such commercials. Here is another case involving a ban on deceptive trade-marking for diet bread. This involved a company that is producing a trade-marked bread, "Lite Diet," which was claimed to have fewer calories than regular bread. Upon investigation, it was found that this bread did have fewer calories per slice, but the reason was that the slice of bread was thinner. If you took the same thickness, it had exactly the same number of calories. In other words, pound for pound, the bread contained the same number of calories as ordinary bread. The suggested qualifying phrases in conjunction with the trademark, the FTC ruled, would completely confuse the public. Hence, the Commission was not satisfied and issued a cease and desist order which was upheld by the Circuit Court of Appeals.

If you think the Federal Trade Commission and the U.S. Department of Justice are the only agencies involved in this, here is something which comes from the U.S. Department of Agriculture. This case came under the Packers and Stockyards Act. Here the Department of Agriculture Judicial Officer ruled that Swift and Company unlawfully sold smoked picnics to The Kroger Company at substantially lower prices than those charged competing retailers, and the discrimination was prohibited. This is but one of many instances in which other agencies besides those two that we normally hear about are helping to put business on a higher legal and hence ethical level.

Now let me refer briefly to the May 14 weekly summary. One of the cases reported here involved the entering of a consent judgment by Volkswagen. Up to this time, Volkswagen prohibited its regular distributors from serving any other make of automobile. Now, according to the consent judgment, the company must notify its regular distributors that they can sell and service other makes of automobiles. The result would have been harsher, no doubt, if the company had not agreed to do this voluntarily. In this summary report is another bread case involving "Hollywood Bread." It involved the same problem as was found with "Lite Diet" bread. "Hollywood Bread" contained fewer calories per slice, merely because it was more thinly sliced. This, obviously did not justify claims that it contained less calories, or that it would reduce weight or prevent its increase.

Here are a couple of cases of interest reported in the May 28 weekly summary. One of them deals with allowances solicited by a supermarket chain for anniversary sales and other special sales events. This violated Section V of the FTC Act, because the company receiving the allowances knew very well that they were not given or made available to anybody else. That was brought out in the testimony, and, therefore, the chain was receiving a discrimination knowingly. By knowingly, we mean it either knew or should have known. In a similar case involving Macy's 100th Anniversary, R. H. Macy and Company received contributions of more than half a million dollars from suppliers to help defray the store's 1958 centennial celebration. Not only did the company solicit and receive such contributions which were not made by suppliers to their other customers, but, allegedly, the company coerced and oppressed suppliers, etc. Now, here are some of the words used in talking about the relationship between legality and ethics. I am going to emphasize some of these words. There was apparently no difficulty in finding that the practice involved coercion or oppression. Who likes to be coerced or oppressed? It is against good morals to do a thing like that. This was certainly an element bringing the solicitations within the traditional concepts of an unfair practice. So you have unfairness, coercion, oppression and all that sort of thing, all of which are indeed unethical as well as illegal. Still another instance involved grocers purchasing cooperatively and receiving brokerage fees. The sellers were ordered just the other day (Central Retail-Owned Grocers, Inc.) to stop that practice. They were deemed to be in violation of the Robinson-Patman Act. Why? Because it involves deception. The law states that brokerage fees are to be given only for services rendered, and it was shown here that the grocers did not render services to those from whom the fees were received. The purchasing cooperative was really representing the buyers, not the sellers, yet the fees were obtained from the sellers. Until the Robinson-Patman Act was passed, that could be done. In fact, the broker could collect double fees if he could get away with it.

Now, what I am driving at is this. Since the legal framework provides the means and guidance for very high ethical standards, then it leads me to my seventh and concluding point. The problem, then, is one of educating businessmen to the nature of this legal framework. We are going to give a whole course in this for our Executive Development Program the last week in August and the first week of September; 10 sessions, an hour and a quarter each. We can not cover this subject adequately in one session of this kind. They are going to get a pretty good insight into what this legal framework is all about, how to interpret it, and how to live within its context. Our problem is mainly one of how to educate business-men as to the nature of this legal framework and the importance of staying within it.—Many businessmen will tell you, we have got to make a living, we have got to meet competition, and they believe they can do anything to achieve those ends. They cannot. The fact of the matter is that they have to stay within the bounds set by this legal framework. To accomplish the latter, they must be imbued with an understanding of the basis for this framework, and have respect for it and not only because of the punitive possibilities when they get caught. That is one of the things, of course. You are a vio-lator of the law, you are a lawbreaker, if you are doing these things that are against it. But businessmen must feel that they should abide by the law because it is fair, right, and just to do so. They have got to understand that, and that means getting a conception of ethics that comes from within. That is one of the objectives, for example in the 300+ trade practice conference rules that have been developed for as many industries, and approved by the Federal Trade Com-mission. I had personal experience in the development of two of those 300+ trade practices conferences. It is something which en-ables businessmen to have a better understanding of what these regulations are all about, and raises the level of morality in business conduct. Thus, I feel that it is the function of education to do this job. It is a most worthy one and one that should be highly rewarding in personal satisfaction.

XII

ETHICS IN MANAGEMENT-COMMUNITY RELATIONS

Paul R. Langdon

An important question facing management concerns the responsibility of the corporation to the community. Sometimes the problem is ignored; at times it is passed over lightly with the thought that people are hired as goods and services are bought. Indifference to peoples' living conditions is rationalized on the ground of not wanting to be paternalistic; therefore, participation in the community is avoided.

I personally think, however, that there is a responsibility of the company to the community. Probably the biggest item in the corporate budget is for salary and wages, and that is for employees. Where employees are concerned, there is often also the sizable factor of fringe benefits, and fringe benefits are very closely related to the community, and to what one is able to offer to the community. In fact, there may be a rather gray area and not a real line of demarcation between the fringe benefits the company offers and what are offered through the community. For example, roads, traffic, schools and type of government—whether the government is a good government—become a problem of the company.

Furthermore, when securing personnel, recruiting people talk about the community in which the company is located and how nice it is. Notice the emphasis on the cultural facilities that are offered in the brochure on working in Columbus, which mentions The Ohio State University, Capital University, and the Art Gallery. Similarly, a brochure published by the state of New York, Department of Commerce, mentions, for instance, that in New York City are New York University and Columbia University and the advantages they afford. The cultural environment in a community is important when it is doing its recruiting.

Conversely, there is the question of responsibility of the company to the community as when a company decides to pick up and leave. A sudden shutdown in the plant affects the whole community, because all of the service industries, the barber shops, the cleaning establishments, the stores, all depend on that company, that company payroll. Another question is the division plant. Some companies take the attitude, when it comes to United Appeals, contributions or drives, that they do not want to donate through a division plant. I think that the corporation must recognize its obligation in the city in which a division plant is located. Corporations must do that which encourages the community to support the corporation, because if the community is not behind the corporation, naturally they are going to take their resentment out and vote against the company if something involves that company.

There are many other ways in which the business corporation is related to the community. I will enumerate a few of them and attempt to show some of the implications involved.

1. Stream pollution—With growing shortage of water, use of streams has been more closely scrutinized. Corporations have been expected to install processes which clean out waste, heretofore pumped into streams. The same is true of air pollution. How should this be viewed by the corporation executive who is trying to meet competition? This was a real problem faced recently by oil refineries in Los Angeles. City officials asked them to shut down for a few days in order to determine if the smog was coming from the refineries. Would you, as the corporation executive, have cooperated in the shutdown? Yet, that would not have proven that the refineries caused the smog, even if it happened to clear at that time; it could have led to an erroneous conclusion—that the operation of the refineries caused the smog.

Of a similar nature was another recent case in Columbus. The school board was planning to build a school building across the railroad tracks from a fertilizer plant. Officials of this plant said to board members: "Please do not place your school here, because you are going to have problems." They were asking the board to put the school somewhere else, but the urban redevelopment program called for a housing project in the vicinity, locating a real concentration of children needing a school there. Corporation officials were anticipating the problem of their relation with the community, foreseeing that the teachers and principals would be complaining when the wind would be coming from a certain direction. Investigation revealed that, for the most part, scrubbers and other equipment could be used to take care of the odors from the plant. The school board went ahead and built the school and to date I have not heard any complaints.

2. *United Appeals*—Another matter involving business-community relations concerns the making of contributions to the United Appeals. Sometimes it is actually less expensive to contribute to a function through the United Appeals, and it may be better than for the government to take it over. Again, I can cite an example drawn from the Columbus area. The state legislature passed a law saying that the school boards must contribute for the training of each retarded child the equivalent of what they charge other school districts for tuition of pupils. They must contribute this amount to the Child Welfare Board, which is under the county. Then the state pays about $250. Previously, that program was handled much on a voluntary basis by the Council for Retarded Children. Parents were being charged for tuition and transportation of pupils, who come from all over the county. But the laws now says that one cannot charge for something that the government is furnishing and so the parents do not pay tuition, nor can they be charged for transportation. Whereas the cost had been quoted as being $600 per pupil, it is now up to $800. This is just one example showing that when a government takes over a function, costs tend to go up and there are fewer contributed services.

3. *Fundamental Research*—Corporations are finding an increasing expectation of the community that they engage in "fundamental research." Actually, there is a great question as to what is "fundamental" and what is "applied" research. However, it is felt that inasmuch as the corporations contribute to science, to the economy, and to the community, they should do more and more fundamental research. This, at least, points up the importance of getting across to the community and to the public just what the corporation is doing.

4. Public Service—With the growing number of public service organizations and quasi-public committees, corporations must consider the extent to which their personnel should become involved in such activities. In connection with this, they should at least know how the personnel of these committees is chosen. For the most part, they are pretty much self-contained or self-perpetuating, with individuals being invited to join. This is generally true of the United Community Council, of community development committees, park commissions, and the like. Representation in Rotary, Kiwanis, the Lions, and other such service organizations also shows that the company officials—management—are interested in the community and in the development of the community. Of course, on their own, employees are encouraged to participate in their own church organizations, in the Scouts, etc.

In connection with this, a question has often been raised as to who in a company should be active in these community relations. Many companies do not face the question until they are asked to have someone serve. They more or less let things take their course in letting the community make the decision. If a request is made, they might indicate that someone would be available, often someone in the field of public relations or employee relations. However, it is better for the company to make its choice before these committees make their own selection of whom they want to serve on their various committees.

5. Jury Duty—Another public service expected of business people is jury duty. It is important that competent business people serve in this capacity, for more reasonable, more responsible verdicts may thereby be expected from our juries. In recent years, insurance companies have been somewhat regarded as fair game by juries. Recently, however, a claim for $50,000 for personal injury was denied because the jury decided that there was no loss for the claimant, although there had been injury, though very slight. This seemed a reasonable verdict by a competent jury. Jury fees, of course, are usually turned into the company if the juror is being paid a wage or salary while he is engaged in that service.

6. Politics—There is an increasing interest in local politics among people in business. The United States Chamber of Commerce has developed a course for aiding those who would participate in politics at the local, county, and state level. Emphasis of this course was on the participation in the party of the individual's choice. It was not saying that one should be Democrat or Republican, but to find out who is the ward chairman and make contact with him. Tell him one is willing to ring doorbells, pass out literature, or do whatever is necessary.

I, personally, question whether a blind following of that course is the answer to the problems. It gives undue emphasis to the *election* of public officers and too little attention to working with those who are already in office. Moreover, corporations are sometimes reluctant to work together in political activities. It is well to become acquainted with officials in the various government organizations so when one does have a problem he can work more effectively with the right person.

There are, of course, some divergencies of viewpoint between the corporations and the politicians. The latter, feeling that they have to satisfy the voters who elected them, believe that they must solve only the current problems. The corporations, on the other hand, are interested in conditions which may be developing five or ten years hence. Another thing, corporations are sometimes sensitive about public reaction to them. For example, in dealing with government offices or officials, companies attempt to avoid giving the impression that they are bringing pressure, particularly by large companies. At the same time, the corporation has a real educational responsibility in getting the role of business profits understood.

Another facet of this question is whether corporations should become actively engaged in politics. Should they support candidates or parties? Obviously, there is an advantage in backing a winner, but the customers of a company are usually among all parties. There is no doubt that with the growing interdependence of government and business, corporations are going to have to take a deeper interest in what is going on. That is more fundamental than just supporting one candidate or another. There is also the question of stockholders' rights against official use of funds in a campaign. What may be sanctioned on small scale, and in one or two instances, may lead to abuses in another case. In general, it seems unwise to endorse a candidate unless some issue is involved that directly affects the corporation. Even then, this may involve more working with government officials in matters concerning laws. Working with officials is often much more effective in achieving an end, for it can be done with some deliberation and resolution of differences. Active open support of candidates and issues, on the other hand, may lead to taking public stands which become subject to much newspaper publicity, and this does not always result in accurate or helpful representation of an interest.

7. *Administrative Differences*—Another ethical question arises in situations where the corporation may feel it has justification to differ with the government in its interpretation of law. The book, *Judgment at Nuremberg*, presents a compelling picture of a situation in which governmental authority and interpretation are questionable. There come times when a corporation must ask itself whether it should blindly follow the government, or whether it should press for acceptance of its own interpretation. For example, in a situation which might be duplicated involving a corporation, the school board recently differed with a state officer on a question involving the relationship of the clerk-treasurer to the Board of Education. The Board has authority to select the superintendent, who recommends the rest of the staff. The law says specifically that the Board shall elect a clerk-treasurer, who holds funds, keeps minutes of the Board, and makes certain financial reports to the State Auditor's office, the State Board of Education, and some others. The Columbus School Board has taken the position that other than where specifically provided by law, the clerk-treasurer shall report to the superintendent. The State Auditor has taken the position that the clerk-treasurer can be required by the Board of Education to do only those things which the law says he must do and nothing more. Fundamentally, I think this is a question of organization, for the clerk-treasurer is very comparable to the corporate treasurer. Suppose that there was a finding of this type concerning a private corporation. The Attorney General has made the ruling and he is attorney for the state. In other words, suppose that the corporate officials had a decision to make which affected profitable management, and the Attorney General said that it was illegal, yet it was good organiza-

tion and good management. In general, in such cases I think one is justified in arguing the differences, so that one does not accept the government decisions blindly.

An ethical consideration in such cases may be whether anyone is hurt by an action which is at variance with official interpretation. Is the taxpayer hurt? One must consider all angles of such situations, but we must accept the standard that the best way of doing something is the best way of doing it, even though it might run directly contrary to certain government officials.

It is apparent from the above illustrations that the answer is not always simple. In conclusion, let me summarize several points which might be useful in formulating policies relating to action in business-community relations:

1. Get all the information you can concerning a situation.

2. Ascertain who would be affected by a decision, and whether anyone would be hurt by it.

3. Base a decision mainly on the long-run effects and implications.

BIBLIOGRAPHY

BOOKS

American Assembly. *Goals for Americans.* Englewood Cliffs, New Jersey: Prentice-Hall, 1960.

An attempt by a Presidential Committee to determine goals and courses of action, to preserve our American way of life. Attention is given to both goals at home and abroad. It is significant to note the importance placed on the individual and the rights of the individual.

American Management Association. *Management's Broadening Responsibilities: A Profile of the Management Job.* New York, 1953.

American Management Association. *Progressive Policies for Business Leadership.* New York, 1952.

Anderson, Thomas J., Jr. *Our Competitive System and Public Policy.* Cincinnati: South Western Publishing Company, 1958.

This is a basic text for courses in the competitive aspects of American economy. The last two chapters are especially good for freshman and sophomore classes.

Andres, Thurman. *Property, Profits, and People.* Washington: Progress Press, 1954.

Anshen, Melvin, and Bach, G. L. *Management and Corporations 1985.* New York: McGraw-Hill Book Company, Inc., 1960. 253 pages.

A collection of the papers presented by renowned industrialists, business educators and social scientists forecasting the corporate scene 25 years hence—with a predominating feeling that the company's role of social responsibility will continue to expand.

Arnold, Thurman. *The Folklore of Capitalism.* New Haven, Connecticut: Yale University Press, 1937.

Barnard, Chester I. *Basic Elements of a Free Dynamic Society.* The Macmillan Company, New York, 1950.

Bartlett, R. W. *The Price of Milk.* Danville, Illinois: Interstate Printers and Publishers, 1941.

This is a historical look at one industry and the pricing of its products. Although somewhat out of date, it does recount the competitive and ethical struggles of the Thirties.

Batchelor, Bronson. *The New Outlook in Business.* New York: Harper & Brothers, 1940.

Baum, Maurice. *Readings in Business Ethics.* Dubuque, Iowa: William C. Brown Company, 1950.

Beard, Miriam. *A History of the Business Man.* New York: The Macmillan Company, 1938.

A historical analysis of the business man and his changing role from the salesman in the Homeric age through the big business man. The businessman's veering course, favoring peace and war, unity and chaos, mystery and science, is portrayed to the conclusion that he obscured himself in history. The democracy of America and the importance of business has forced the business man to go "in search of credo and character."

Beck, R. N. *The Meaning of Americanism.* New York: Philosophical Library, 1956.

Beckman, Theodore N., and Davidson, William R. *Marketing, Seventh Edition.* New York: The Ronald Press, 1962. (Chapter 34, "Legal Impact upon Marketing.")

An extensive appraisal of government's impact on marketing, concentrating on its general impact upon domestic marketing activities of competitive business enterprises, and including an exploration of the philosophical bases of the laws governing marketing activity.

Bendix, Reinhard. *Work and Authority in Industry: Ideologies of Management in the Course of Industrialization.* New York: John Wiley and Sons, 1956.

Bennett, John; Bowen, Howard; Brown, William Jr.; and Oxnam, G. Bromley. *Christian Values and Economic Life.* New York: Harper and Brothers, Publishers, 1954. 263 pages.

A discussion by the authors on some aspects of the economic problem, in particular that in the United States; an attempt to obtain some relationship with world trade is made. Christian values of ethics and morals are tied in with the above ideas. A good discussion on the economic goals of life as compared with the Christian ideals was presented.

Bennett, John C. *Christian Ethics and Social Policy.* New York: Charles Scribner's Sons, 1946.

Benoit, Emile. *Ethical Issues in the Economic Impact of Defense Spending and Disarmament.* Department of the Church and Economic Life, Division of Christian Life and Work, National Council of Churches of Christ in the U.S.A., 1960.

Disarmament has basic aspects in negotiations for universal lessening of tensions on the international level. This paper deals with ethical issues arising out of economic impact not only of present defense spending, but, primarily, of possible disarmament in the future.

Berger, Morrow; Abel, Theodore; and Page, Charles H. (eds.). *Freedom and Control in Modern Society.* Princeton, New Jersey: D. Van Nostrand Company, 1954.

Berle, Adolph A., Jr. *The Twentieth Century Capitalist Revolution.* New York: Harcourt, Brace and Company, 1954.

The study of the modern corporation as a political institution forced to operate within the framework of a democratic society.

Berle, Adolph A., Jr., and Means, Gardner C. *The Modern Corporation and Private Property.* New York: The Macmillan Company, 1933.

Boulding, Kenneth E. *The Organizational Revolution: A Study in the Ethics of Economic Organization.* New York: Harper and Brothers, 1953.

Bowen, Howard R. *Social Responsibilities of the Businessman.* New York: Harper and Bros., 1953.

A systematic study of the businessman's concept of his social responsibilities. The author finds that today's businessmen are more concerned than were their predecessors about their social responsibility. The reason is three-fold: They have been forced to be more concerned, they have been persuaded to be more concerned, and, owing largely to the separation of ownership and control in large corporations, conditions have been favorable to the development of this concern.

Brady, R. A. *Business as a System of Power.* New York: Columbia University Press, 1943.

Braibanti, Ralph, and Spengler, Joseph J. (eds.). *Tradition, Values, and Socio-Economic Development.* Durham, North Carolina: Duke University Press, 1961.

Britt, Steuart H. *The Spenders.* New York: McGraw-Hill Book Co., Inc., 1961. Chapter IX.

Discussion of position of present day business as the servant of the consumer. Indicates the way marketing through promotion and advertising helps consumers in various manners by discussing the relationships of prices and buying. Also refers to the importance of marketing research in relation to satisfying the wants and needs of the consumers or spenders.

Brooks, John Graham. *The Conflict Between Private Monopoly and Good Citizenship.* Cambridge: The Riverside Press Company, 1909.

Buckingham, Walter. *Automation: Its Impact on Business and People.* New York: Harper and Brothers, 1961. 190 pages.

An extensive explanation of the nature, extent, and implications of automation, with strong suggestion that preparation for the new force includes planning for the adjustment of workers to new conditions and for the rehabilitation of those becoming unemployed.

Bullis, Harry A. *A Businessman Views a Changing World.* Minneapolis: General Mills, 1952.

Bunting, Earl, and Maker, Edward. *They Want to Know: Answers from Business to Questions All the American People Are Asking.* New York: Farrar, Strauss, and Young, 1952.

Bunting, J. Whitney (ed.). *Ethics for Modern Business Practice.* New York: Prentice-Hall, Inc., 1953.

A brief analysis and definition of ethics, plus a report of business ethics as they are or should be in various parts of business. The author also indicates the trend ethics is taking.

Burnham, James. *The Managerial Revolution.* New York: John Day Company, 1941.

Burr, Nelson R. *A Critical Bibliography of Religion in America.* Volume 4, parts 3, 4 and 5. Princeton, New Jersey: Princeton University Press, 1961. pp. 545–1219.

This series looks at many aspects of religion. It will be a valuable reference book for one working with religion in any way.

Bursk, Edward C. (ed.). *Business and Religion: A New Dimension in Management.* New York: Harper and Brothers, 1959.

A group of studies stimulated by the *Harvard Business Review*, bring together the thinking of twelve business executives, teachers and theologians on the subject of business and religion. They blend religious, scientific, psychological, and philosophical insights, pointing ways to realize ethical ideals in the business world. Guidelines are presented by which the businessman can move a step beyond the considerations of physical and social needs toward objectives which stimulate creativity and are spiritually satisfying as well.

Cabot, Richard C. *Adventures on the Borderlands of Ethics.* New York: Harper and Brothers, 1926. (Chapter 3.)

The author cites the fact that businessmen very often sheer away from questions of ethics and take refuge in the realm of custom, legality, or of personal feeling. He further cites that this practice is not only related to businessmen but also to teachers, doctors, and social workers.

Cahn, E. N. *The Moral Decision.* Bloomington, Indiana: Indiana University Press, 1955.

Cahn analyzes key cases in law in order to demonstrate that moral guides can be found in American judicial decisions.

Calhoun, George M. *The Ancient Greeks and the Evolution of Standards in Business.* Cambridge: The Riverside Press Company, 1926.

Cartwright, Dorwin. *Studies in Social Power.* Ann Arbor, Michigan: University of Michigan Press, 1959.

Power is viewed as the ability of one person (or group) to influence or control some aspect of another person (or group). The studies deal with such phenomena as the ability of one person to influence the attitudes and behavior of another, the abilities of individuals to influence the decision of a group, and the ability of one person to determine whether or not another reaches his goal. The book includes a chapter on power as a neglected variable in social psychology. The closing chapters are concerned with the theory of social power and include the formulation of a rigorous mathematical model of power.

Chase, Stuart; Ruttenberg, Stanley H.; Nourse, Edwin G.; and Given, William B., Jr. *The Social Responsibility of Management.* New York: School of Commerce, Accounts, and Finance, New York University, 1950.

Childs, Marquis W., and Cater, Douglas. *Ethics in a Business Society.* New York: Harper and Brothers, 1954.

A description of how the individual may find himself in today's society with the large corporations. It also deals with the evolution of today's business ethics, the economic forces plus labor, church, government and business having a variety of motives and objectives, attaining a balance among mixed objectives in a free and mixed economy.

Chisholm, George Brock. *Social Responsibility.* New York: Association Press, 1948.

Clark, John M. *Alternative to Serfdom.* New York: Alfred A. Knopf, 1948.

Five lectures delivered at the University of Michigan, 1947. Man needs to belong to a community unit smaller and more personal than the overpowering state; but the units that meet this—including trade unions—are not parts of an integrated community, but monopolistic groups, at war with each other. To resolve these conflicts without destroying liberty requires that the powers of these groups be fairly well balanced and that they be responsibly exercised.

————. *Economic Institutions and Human Welfare*. New York: Alfred A. Knopf, 1957.

————. *The Ethical Basis of Economic Freedom*. Westport, Connecticut: Kazanjian Economic Foundation, 1955.

————. *Guideposts in Times of Change*. New York: Harper and Brothers, 1949.

A statement of the objectives of our economy within the framework of mass production and group power. An attempt is made to apply common sense to economic theory through the "principle of strategic decision." Technical discussions of the economic mechanism deal with methods of sustaining the flow of purchasing and attacks the problem of the effect of the structure of prices and wages on the total volume of production and employment. We are in the era of transition, one in which it is impossible to return to past standards of "normalcy."

Cochran, T. C. *The American Business System: A Historical Perspective, 1900–1955*. Cambridge, Massachusetts: Harvard University Press, 1957.

————. *Basic History of American Business*. Princeton, New Jersey: D. Van Nostrand Company, 1959.

Commager, Henry S. *The American Mind*. New Haven, Connecticut: Yale University Press, 1950.

Cordiner, Ralph J. *New Frontiers for Professional Managers*. New York: McGraw-Hill Book Company, Inc., 1956.

Coser, Lewis A. *The Functions of Social Conflict*. London: Routledge and Kegan Paul, Ltd., 1956.

The author provides an excellent clarification of the concept of social conflict. Through an examination of a number of propositions distilled from theories of social conflict, and in particular from the work of Georg Simmel, attention is called to the conditions under which social conflict may contribute to the maintenance, adjustment, or adaptation of social relationships and social structures. In the examination of the sixteen propositions set forth by Coser, the reader will find many ideas having important implications for various areas of human activity.

Cronin, Rev. J. F. *Catholic Social Principles*. Milwaukee: Bruce Publishing Company, 1951.

A good reference source on the medieval period, the church and the social problem, and man and economic life. Points out the Catholic point of view and cites quotations from the past Popes.

Cuber, John F., and Harper, Robert A. *Problems of American Society: Values in Conflict*. New York: Henry Holt & Company, 1948.

Curti, M. *The Growth of American Thought*. New York: Harper and Brothers, 1943.

Cutlip, Scott M., and Center, Allen H. *Effective Public Relations*. New York: Prentice-Hall, 1952. pp. 70–73.

A description of the role of mass media in molding public opinion and the implications for the practice of public relations.

Dale, Ernest. *The Great Organizers*. New York: McGraw-Hill Book Company, Inc., 1960.

A study of the contributions to corporate organization and ethical practice made by such pioneers as the DuPonts, Sloane, and Westinghouse, concluding with an expression of concern over the lack of control which exists under today's managerial system.

Dalton, Melville. *Men Who Manage.* New York: John Wiley and Sons, Inc., 1959.

Using the participant-observer research approach, Dalton provides new and enlightening observations on the "nonofficial" behavior within organizations. He analyzes a number of commercial and industrial firms, including several factories, a drug chain, a department store, and a research firm. His method provides additional evidence for the frequently made observation that formal social systems provide imprecise guides for action and for the prediction of behavior.

Davis, Ralph C. *Fundamentals of Top Management.* New York: Harper and Brothers, 1951. (Chapter 4.)

Davis discusses practical values of ethical standards, the function of ethics in business, and a brief discussion of the primarily legal basis of ethics in business.

Demant, V. A. *Religion and The Decline of Capitalism.* New York: Charles Scribner's Sons, 1949.

Viewing contemporary capitalism as a sociological abnormality, Demant argues that capitalism achieved great economic advantages at the cost of colossal social dislocations. However, our self-regulating market society never existed in its entirety and has been declining since the 19th century.

Dennison, Henry S. *Ethics and Modern Business.* Boston: Houghton Mifflin, 1932.

Dennison, Henry S., and Galbraith, John K. *Modern Competition and Public Policy.* New York: Oxford University Press, 1938.

Dewey, Robert E., *et al* (ed.). *Problems of Ethics.* New York: The Macmillan Company, 1961.

Readings from various philosophers organized topically. It is written as a text for a problem-centered ethics course. The book is divided into three sections—preliminary problems, the search for a moral standard, and the analytical approach to ethics.

Dimock, Marshal E. *Bureaucracy and Trusteeship in Large Corporations.* Washington: Temporary National Economic Committee, 1940.

————. *Free Enterprise and the Administrative State.* University Station, Alabama: Alabama University Press, 1951.

Dirlam, Joel B., and Kahn, Alfred E. *Fair Competition, The Law and Economics of Antitrust Policy.* Ithaca, New York: Cornell University Press, 1954.

The authors view antitrust laws as our economic Magna Charta, helping to explain the superiority of the American economy. They criticize not the Sherman Act but the excessively doctrinaire, legalistic, economically naive interpretations originated by the enforcement agencies that have been unnecessary and require reconsideration in the light of new economic conceptions of workable competition, recognizing pure competition to be both unattainable and undesirable, there being an optimum balance between number of buyers and number of sellers.

Drucker, Peter F. *Landmarks of Tomorrow*. New York: Harper and Brothers, 1959.

————. *The New Society*. New York: McGraw-Hill Book Company, Inc., 1952.

Duff, Edward S. J. *The Social Thought of the World Council of Churches*. New York: Association Press, 1956.

Edel, May and Abraham. *Anthropology and Ethics*. Springfield, Illinois: Charles C. Thomas, 1959.

Anthropologists believe there is no simple set of common moral principles but widely different sets of virtues and goals, ideals and standards, operating in terms of different kinds of economic institutions which have grown up to fill this need.

Edwards, Corwin D. *Big Business and the Policy of Competition*. Cleveland: Western Reserve University Press, 1956.

A somewhat critical look at big business because of its tremendous competitive power. The importance of competition in the United States is stressed, and the necessity of insuring that competition involving businesses of large sizes be tempered and controlled appropriate to the public interest is explored.

————. *Maintaining Competition: Requisites of a Governmental Policy*. New York: McGraw-Hill Book Company, Inc., 1949.

Investigation of governmental policy with respect to maintaining of effective competition in American business. Cites difficulties encountered today due to concentration of economic power by a few large companies. Shows ineffectiveness of many present laws in curbing collusion and restrictive agreements.

Eells, Richard, *Corporation Giving in a Free Society*. New York: Harper and Brothers, 1956.

————. *The Meaning of Modern Business*. New York: Columbia University Press, 1959.

Eells, Richard, and Walton, Clarence. *Conceptual Foundations of Business,* Homewood, Illinois: Richard D. Irwin, 1961.

Elliott, Osborn. *Men at the Top*. New York: Harper and Brothers, 1959. 236 pages.

An in-depth study of the on-and-off-the-job behavior patterns of some of the leading chief executives of American business, revealing on the part of most a genuine concern for social responsibility.

The Ethical Problems in Relations of Business to Government. New York: The Ronald Press Company, 1932.

A series of lectures delivered in 1931 on the William A. Vawter Foundation on Business Ethics, Northwestern University School of Commerce. Speakers and their lectures are listed:

1. Klein, J. "Factors in Business Behavior."

Codes do not create standards of good behavior, they just record them. Business ethics are developed, they are not made simply by neatly written phrases.

2. Humphrey, W. E. "Business Ethics and the Federal Trade Commission." The most effective way to protect the public and the honest competitor is to help business to help itself in removing unfair and misleading practices.
3. Van der Vries, J. V. *"Collective Business: Its Methods and Objectives."* Presents 15 principles of good business conduct.
4. Donald, W. J. "The Management Point of View." Presents 5 criteria of what constitutes a management profession.

Fagothey, Austin. *Right and Reasons Ethics in Theory and Practice.* St. Louis: C. V. Mosby Company, 1959.

An examination of ethics from the Aristotelian-Thomistic approach. The text is general in coverage. Chapter 30 deals with "Work and Wages" and the responsibility of parties to a wage contract.

Fanfani, A. *Catholicism, Protestantism, and Capitalism.* New York: Sheed and Ward, May, 1935.

Excellent reading, present early history of catholicism and capitalism, and the protestant reformation and capitalism.

Federal Council of Churches. *The Church and Economic Life: Basic Christian Principles and Assumptions.* New York, 1948.

Federick, J. G. *Book of Business Standards.* New York: Nicholas L. Brown, 1925.

The author defines standards by the use of which business decisions can be made.

Fenn, Dan H. (ed.). *Business Responsibility in Action.* New York: McGraw-Hill Book Company, Inc., 1959.

Filipetti, George. *Industrial Management in Transition.* Homewood, Illinois: Richard D. Irwin, 1953.

Finn, David. *Public Relations and Management.* New York: Reinhold Publishing Corporation, 1960.

A description of how the public relations function fits into management— important to the study of ethics because it quashes some of the exaggerated claims regarding the efficacy of public relations practice, and deplores some of the questionable practices done under the guise of public relations.

Fitch, John A. *Social Responsibilities of Labor.* New York: Harper and Brothers, 1957.

A look at the responsibilities of the labor movement in our complex society.

Fletcher, J. (ed). *Christianity and Property.* Philadelphia, Pennsylvania: The Westminster Press, 1947.

Flubacher, Joseph F. *The Concept of Ethics in the History of Economics.* New York: Vantage Press, 1950.

Forbush, Dascomb R. *Management's Relationships with its Publics.* Evanston, Illinois: School of Business, Northwestern University, 1960.

Fromm, Erich. *Man for Himself.* New York: Rinehart and Company, Inc., 1947. 250 pages.

The author discusses some of the bases of ethics through the explanation of man's characteristics. Ethical problems as related to these characteristics, after some psychological and philosophical analyses, were discussed.

The Function of Management in American Life. Stanford, California: Graduate School of Business, Stanford, University, 1948.

Galbraith, John K. *The Affluent Society.* Boston: Houghton Mifflin, 1958.
Galbraith's criticism of existing ideas and attitudes in economics, showing how existing economic ideas were fashioned for a world very different from our own.

————. *American Capitalism: The Concept of Countervailing Power.* Boston: Houghton Mifflin, 1952.

Garnett, Christopher B. Jr. *Wisdom in Conduct.* New York: Harcourt, Brace and Company, 1940. 420 pages.
Basis of discussion is an ethical theory called wisdom of conduct. Also, some of the concepts that are for and against this theory were introduced. Application of the theory to some of the ethical problems and their relationship to psychology and philosophy.

Gibney, Frank. *The Operators.* New York: Harper and Brothers, 1960.
A discussion of the extent to which the "fast buck" approach to modern society has evolved. The author attempts to show that we are headed toward a moral collapse if it is not recognized and corrected.

Glover, John D. *The Attack on Big Business.* Boston: Graduate School of Business Administration, Harvard University, 1954.

Golden, Clinton S., and Ruttenberg, Harold J. *Dynamics of Industrial Democracy.* New York: Harper and Brothers, 1942.

Goldsen, Rose K.; Rosenberg, Morris; Williams, Robin M. Jr.; and Suchman, Edward A. *What College Students Think.* Princeton, N. J.: D. Van Nostrand Co., Inc., 1960. (Chapter 2).
A description of the mental world of American college students arrived at by empirical social research. A report of the more general findings of a research program conducted by the Cornell Values Study with proofs mainly based on statistical correlations. The study depends upon internal consistency of the analysis for validation. Eleven universities participated and were selected as the most influential.

Gordon, Robert A. *Business Leadership in the Large Corporation.* Washington Brookings Institution, 1945.

Gorer, Geoffrey. *The American People: A Study in National Character.* New York: W. W. Norton, 1948.

Goyder, George. *The Future of Private Enterprise: A Study in Responsibility.* Oxford, England: B. Blackwell, 1951.

Graham, Frank D. *Social Goals and Economic Institutions.* Princeton, New Jersey: Princeton University Press, 1942.

Greene, Theodore M. *Our Cultural Heritage.* Houston, Texas: Elsenier Press, 1956.

Greenewalt, Crawford H. *The Uncommon Man: The Individual in the Organization.* New York: McGraw-Hill Book Company, Inc. 1959.

Griffin, Clare E. *Enterprise in a Free Society.* Homewood, Illinois: Richard D. Irwin, 1949.

Griswold, Glenn, and Griswold, Denney. *Your Public Relations.* New York: Funk and Wagnalls Company, 1948.
A Handbook prepared by authorities in various public relations areas.

Haldane, R. B. Life of Adam Smith. London: Walter Scott, 1887.
A review of Smith's life with frequent mention of his *Wealth of Nations*. Haldane shows Smith as a moralist, an economist, and his relations to politics.
Harbrecht, Paul P., and Berle, Adolph A., Jr., *Toward the Paraproprietal Society*. New York: Twentieth Century Fund, 1959.
Harlow, Rex, and Black, Marvin M. *Practical Public Relations*. New York: Harper and Brothers, 1947. pp. 196-219.
A discussion on the foundations, divisions, applications and practices of the practical public relations, and their importance.
Heermance, Edgar L. *Can Business Govern Itself*. New York: Harper and Brothers, 1933.
Codes of Ethics, Burlington, Vermont: Free Press, 1924.
A collection of ethical codes from professions and trades presented to facilitate the work of association officers in drafting or revising standards, to bring before leaders of public opinion the concrete evidences of a remarkable ethical movement, and to assemble case material for those whose study of Ethics wish to make use of the laboratory methods.
The Ethics of Business. New Haven, Conn: Harper and Brothers, 1926.
To present the standards of conduct in business and the reason for them. Also an introduction to the study of Social Ethics.
Heilbroner, Robert. *The Future as History*. New York: Harper and Brothers, 1960.
———. *The Wordly Philosophers*. New York: Simon and Schuster, 1953.
This book tells the views of economists in observing people's drives for wealth. This is a good book to help one learn some of the history behind many ethical problems in existence today.
Heilbroner, Robert L., and Strieter, Paul. *The Great Economists*. London: Eyre and Spottisswoode, 1955.
The American way of life under capitalism as viewed by several economists. A comparison between this and some of the other systems, such as socialism, Marxism, etc. Some ideas from other known economists presented with respect to capitalism.
Heyel, Carl. (ed). *Handbook of Industrial Research Management*. New York: Reinhold Publishing Corporation, 1960.
Chapter 6, "Patents" relates the business and legal considerations affecting patents in order that policies can be set and administered. Failure of communications where patents are involved is common. Deceptive oversimplification and imbalance of short-term and long-term goals can be costly. If the intertwined legal and business aspects of patents are to be profitably analyzed, management must be knowledgeable and perceptive in both areas.
Hodges, Wayne. *Company and Community*. New York: Harper and Brothers, 1958. 360 pages.
A detailed study of business and industrial community relations activity in Syracuse, New York, with a substantiated conclusion that a planned, ongoing community relations program can contribute mightily to building and maintaining a favorable community climate of opinion.

Hourani, George F. *Ethical Value.* Ann Arbor, Michigan: University of Michigan Press, 1956.

Houser, Theodore V. *Big Business and Human Values.* New York: McGraw-Hill Book Company, Inc., 1957. 103 pages.
An exposition of how big business must and can apply human values in its relationships with employees, as well as its claimant "publics"—community, stockholders, government, customers, competitors; and in its overseas operations.

Hoyt, Elizabeth; McConnell, Joseph; Hooks, Janet; and Reid, Margaret. *American Income and Its Use.* New York: Harper and Brothers, 1954.

Hurff, George B. *Social Aspects of Enterprise in a Large Corporation.* Philadelphia: University of Pennsylvania Press, 1950.

Hutchinson, John A. *Faith, Reason, Existence.* New York: Oxford University Press, 1956. Hutchinson sees ethics as historically and necessarily based upon religion wherein the end of man is the active service of God, a service not apart from but in and through his life in society.

Johnson, F. Ernest, and Holt, Arthur E. *Christian Ideals in Industry.* New York: The Methodist Book Concern, 1924.

Johnson, F. Ernest and Ackerman, J. Amory, *The Church as Employer, Money Raiser, and Investor.* New York: Harper and Brothers, 1959.

Johnson, Harold L. *Exploration in Responsible Business Behavior: An Exercise in Behavioral Economics.* Atlanta, Georgia: School of Business Administration, Georgia State College of Business Administration, 1958.

Johnston, Herbert. *Business Ethics.* New York: Pitman Publishing Company, 1956.
Johnston discusses the ethical considerations of business concerning man, government, unions, and the public. The Roman Catholic viewpoint on these areas is presented.

Jordan, Elijah. *Business Be Damned.* New York: Henry Schuman, Inc., 1952.
A bitter tirade against the worst in businessmen.

Kallen, Horace M. *Cultural Pluralism and the American Idea,* Philadelphia: University of Pennsylvania Press, 1956.

Kaplan, Abraham D. H. *Big Enterprise in a Competitive System.* Washington: Brookings Institution, 1953.

Kapp, K. W. *The Social Costs of Private Enterprise.* Cambridge, Massachusetts: Harvard University Press, 1950.

Kelso, Louis D., and Adler, Mortimer J., Jr. *The Capitalist Manifesto* New York: Random House, 1958.

Kerr, Clark; Dunlop, John T.; Harbison, Frederick; and Myers, Charles A. *Industrialism and Industrial Man: The Problem of Labor and Management and Economic Growth.* Cambridge, Massachusetts: Harvard University Press, 1960.

Kierkgaard, Soren. *Fear and Trembling.* Princeton, New Jersey; Princeton Press, 1941.
Analysis of the relationships between Abraham and Isaac of the Bible and the relationship between Abraham and God. A searching investigation of the ethical questions involved in these relationships.

Knight, Frank H., and Merriam, Thornton W. *The Economic Order and Religion*. New York: Harper and Brothers, 1945.
The main theme deals with criticism not directed against Christian ethics specifically but against broader principles of moralism—the idea that goodness alone, will solve our social problems.
—————. *The Ethics of Competition*. New York: Harper and Brothers, 1935.
Business decisions and their effect on the system of competition. In this relation, there is a discussion of the wants of people and the creation of values. Personal wants cannot lead to values, as people do not regard wants as an ultimate.
—————. *Freedom and Reform*. New York: Harper and Brothers, 1947.
Knudson, Albert C. *The Principles of Christian Ethics,* New York: Abingdon-Cokesbury Press, 1958.
A systematic and critical exposition of Christian ethics in the light of its history and of present-day thought. Special attention is devoted to the fundamental principles of the Christian ethic.
Lane, Robert E. *The Regulation of Businessmen*. New Haven, Connecticut: Yale University Press, 1954.
Laski, Harold J. *The American Democracy*. New York: Viking Press, 1948.
Lerner, Max. *America as a Civilization*. New York: Simon and Schuster, 1957.
An analysis and interpretation of the American way of life. In studying what Lerner calls the "American experience," the author considers history, culture, people, economy, politics, society, art, and world power of the United States.
Letts, Harold C. *Christian Action in Economic Life*. Philadelphia: Muhlenberg Press, 1953.
Leys, W. A. R. *Ethics for Business Decisions*. New York: Prentice-Hall, Inc., 1952.
Lilienthal, David E. *Big Business: A New Era*. New York: Harper and Brothers, 1953.
Lippman, Walter. *The Good Society*. Boston: Little, Brown and Company, 1937.
It is important for our country to have liberalism in order to have a rising standard of living, freedom and good education. On the other hand, collectivism can be the country's downfall.
—————. *The Public Philosophy*. New York: The American Library of the World Literature, Inc., 1955. An examination of the decline of modern democracies, essentially explained in light of the fact that they have abandoned the main concepts, principles, precepts, and the general manner of thinking which the author terms the public philosophy. The author feels that an acceptable public philosophy is requisite in any long-term successful democratic society. The idea is offered that a revival of the fundamental public philosophy is long overdue.
Litchfield, P. W. *Autumn Leaves Reflections of an Industrial Lieutenant*. Cleveland: The Corday and Gross Co., 1945.
The author gives three principles to bring happiness to the individual and progress to the nation:

1. to be guided by the teachings of Christ, which call for honoring and serving God and your fellow man.
2. to find a creed which to your mind best fits these principles, and accept it fully and sincerely.
3. having selected a particular faith, embrace it with a determination to get the fullest possible value out of its accumulated strength and traditions.

Lodge, Rupert. *Philosophy of Business*. Chicago: University of Chicago Press, 1945.

Lord, Everett W., *The Fundamentals of Business Ethics*. New York: Ronald Press, 1926.

Presents the principles of honor, truth and universal service, to make them more definite. An orderly and undogmatic presentation of the moral standards of present day business life.

Lundborg, Louis. *Public Relations in the Local Community*. New York: Harper and Brothers, 1950.

A book concentrating on good and ethical practices of the functions of public relations in the local community.

MacGibbon, Elizabeth Gregg. *Manners in Business*. New York: The MacMillan Company, 1944.

Practical suggestions for conduct in the business world—aimed primarily at the female office worker.

March, J. G., and Simon, H. A. *Organizations*. New York: Wiley and Sons, 1959.

A comprehensive book about the theory of formal organizations. The authors feel the subject is more significant than the world has acknowledged. In modern social science, in fact, the subject does occupy a rather insignificant place and for this reason existing literature is examined and criticized. The examination centers on the propositions about organizational behavior grouped under: 1) organization members being passive instruments, 2) incomplete parallelism between personal goals and organization goals and 3) members as decision makers and problem solvers.

Using these models as the primary basis for sorting out propositions and organizing existing knowledge a thorough coverage is made giving consideration to some psychological postulates which are basic to some of the salient characteristics of human behavior in organizations. An excellent bibliography is included.

Marias, Julian. *Reason and Life*. London, England: Hollis and Carter, 1956.

A writing on the interplay of reason and logical thinking and the purpose of life, considering the part played by religion in life.

Maritain, Jacques. *The Person and the Common Good*. New York: Charles Scribner's Sons, 1947.

A philosophical inquiry into the role of the individual in society.

Mascall, E. L. *Christian Theology and Natural Science*. New York: Longmans, Green, and Company, 1956.

A book concerned with natural science and scientific thinking and their effects on Christian theology, more specifically, theistic ethics.

Maslow, Abraham H. (ed.). *New Knowledge in Human Values;* Harper and Brothers, 1959.

Mason, Edward S. (ed.). *The Corporation in Modern Society.* Cambridge: Harvard University Press, 1959.
A collection of fourteen articles by well known contributors, together with a foreword by A. A. Berle. Deals with the corporation's place in society.

Maurer, Herrymon. *Great Enterprise: Growth and Behavior of the Big Corporation.* New York: The Macmillan Company, 1955.

May, Henry F. *Protestant Churches and Industrial America.* New York: Harper and Brothers, 1949.
An investigation of the position and power of protestantism as it faced the issues brought about by large-scale industrialism in the late nineteenth century.

Mazur, P. *The Standards We Raise.* New York: Harper and Brothers, 1953
Mazur discusses the success of the American economy and its characteristics and attributes such a vital economy to rejecting the inevitabliliy of a saturation of desire and to making purchases in the domestic market possible in one way or another.

Merrill, Harwood F. (ed.). *The Responsibilities of Business Leadership.* Cambridge, Mass.: Harvard University Press, 1949.
The many ideas presented in this book boil down, in the end, to one: that if one acts toward others as he would want them to act toward him, then he will be on the right road toward discharging his business responsibilities.

Messner, J. *Social Ethics.* St. Louis: B. Herder Book Company, 1949.

Mills, C. Wright. *The Power Elite.* New York: Oxford University Press, 1956.
A study of people who occupy strategic places in American society. The very rich, the corporate executives, political leaders and the military leaders are in a position to make decisions which can affect our country and the world. Mills believes that the top of the American system of power is highly unified and more powerful than the fragmented bottom.

————. *White Collar: The American Middle Class.* New York: Oxford University Press, 1951.
Although the U.S. has been transformed from a nation of small capitalists to a nation of hired employees, the ideology of the former still persists. The increasing routinization, standardization and collectivation of jobs held by the New Middle Class has generated political indifference, lack of aspiration and a culture of resignation.

Monjar, H. B. *Code of Ethics.* New York: The Key Publishing Company, Inc., 1938. 193 pages.
A series of articles of the code of ethics as viewed by the author. A complete analysis on the human character and traits with respect to establishing this code of ethics.

Mooney, James D. *The New Capitalism.* New York: The Macmillan Company, 1934.

Morison, Elting E. (ed.). *The American Style.* New York: Harper and Brothers, 1958.

Muelder, Walter G. *Foundations of the Responsible Society.* New York: Abington Press, 1959.

―――――. *Religion and Economic Responsibility*. New York: Charles Scribner's Sons, 1953.

Munier, J. D. *Some American Approximations to Pius XI's "Industries and Professions."* Washington, D. C.: The Catholic University of America Press, 1943.

Good reading for an historical review of the railroad industry, the bituminous coal industry, industry committees, and the national war labor board.

Myrdal, Gunnar. *An American Dilemma*. New York: Harper and Brothers, 1944.

Nell-Bruening, O. Von. *Reorganization of Social Economy*. Milwaukee: Bruce Publishing Company, 1936.

Niebuhr, Reinhold. *Faith and History*. London, England: James Nisbet and Company, Ltd., 1949.

Traces the effect of history, primarily the seventeenth century scientific revolution, on faith and its relative strengths compared to other criteria of value.

―――――. *Moral Man and Immoral Society*. New York: Charles Scribner's Sons, 1932.

A sharp distinction must be made between the moral and social behavior of individuals and of social groups, national, racial, and economic; and that this distinction justifies and necessitates political policies which a purely individualistic ethic must always find embarrassing.

Niebuhr, H. R. *Social Sources of Denominationalism*. 51 Caroline Street, Hamden, Connecticut: The Shoestring Press, 1954.

Northcutt, Clarence H. *Christian Principles in Industry*. London, England: Sir Isaac Pitman & Sons, 1958.

Nosow, Sigmund, and Form, William H. (ed.). *Man, Work, and Society*. New York: Basic Books, Inc., 1962.

This book brings together a comprehensive collection of writings in the sociology of occupations. Anthropology, economics, and psychology are also drawn upon. Five major themes are covered: the nature of work, unemployment, and leisure; occupational structure; details about individual occupations; the way in which occupational structure and individual occupations mesh with other elements of society; and the use of particular occupations as clues to broader social problems. Suggested is that perhaps the most important sociological generalization of our day will be concerned with dynamics of cultural change and the patterns of relationship between diverse cultural systems. The future is directed toward the development of the non-industrial countries of the world and this is engulfing Western society. Occupational systems must be understood in the perspective of this emerging world order.

Nourse, Edwin G. *Price-Making in a Democracy*. Washington: Brookings Institution, 1944.

Obenhaus, Victor. *The Responsible Christian*. Chicago: University of Chicago Press, 1957.

O'Connor, R. *Gould's Millions*. New York: Doubleday, 1961.

An interesting biography although it is wordy and sensationalized. However, one does find that Gould has management by objectives. His objectives in most every case seemed to be *money*.

Owens, Richard N. *Business Management and Public Policy*. Homewood, Illinois: Richard D. Irwin, Inc., 1958.

A detailed analysis of the problems of management in attempting to serve the various groups with their conflicting objectives. The problem of the government in determining public policy is to determine the nature and extent of public control over private enterprise. Management needs the freedom to manage, but it cannot be permitted to make tyrannical use of the great power that it possesses. The problem of business management is to operate the enterprise efficiently and to maintain its financial strength. At the same time, management must deal fairly with stockholders, customers, management personnel, employees, labor unions, competitors, suppliers, and the general public.

Packard, Vance. *The Status Seekers*. New York: Pocket Books, Inc., 1959.

An examination of the class structure within our society. The author discusses the various class symbols, such as car, home, church, and school, and develops the idea that our society is highly stratified, in spite of the traditional views to the contrary. A critical look at society's rules and limitations on individual freedom in all areas of contemporary endeavor.

Page, Edward D. *Trade Morals, Their Origin, Growth and Province*. New Haven: Yale University Press, 1914.

The book is an outgrowth of lectures to seniors at Yale. In essence, it is a sociological lecture on business, how it got that way, and how it is likely to change. Quite a different view from that expressed today.

Parrington, Vernon L. *Main Currents in American Thought*. New York: Harcourt, Brace and Company, 1956.

Parsons, Talcott, and Smelser, N. J. *Economy and Society*. Glencoe, Illinois: Free Press, 1956.

Pask, Gordon. *An Approach to Cybernetics*. New York: Harper and Brothers, 1961.

Chapter 8 deals with industrial cybernetics—its impact, the structure of industry, and decision making. Cybernetics offers a scientific approach to the "cussedness" of organisms, suggests how their behaviors can be catalysed and the "mystique" and rule of thumb banished. With structural changes from automation there will be added efficiency of the process with an assumed social responsibility on the part of management. Decisions by teamwork or system evolutionary networks are suggested as possibilities.

Peck, William G. *A Christian Economy*. New York: The Macmillan Company, 1954.

Pepper, Stephan C. *The Sources of Value*. Los Angeles: University of California Press, 1958.

A principal finding in this empirical study of values is that the guiding concept linking successive levels of values is a selective system, which is a peculiar dynamic structure which allows one to describe errors as occurring within the system by virtue of the fact that these errors are corrected by the dynamics of the system itself. A selective system operates to eliminate errors and accumulates correct results in terms of criteria embodied in the system.

Perry, Ralph B. *The Moral Economy.* New York: Charles Scribner's Sons, 1909.

————. *Realms of Value.* Cambridge, Massachusetts: Harvard University Press, 1954.

Polanyi, Karl. *The Great Transformation.* New York: Farrar and Rinehart, 1944.

Pope Leo XIII. *Rerum Novarum.* New York: Paulist Press, 1891.
  On the social responsibilities of Capital and Labor:
  1. Market wage not necessarily a just wage.
  2. Gave guarded blessing to labor union.
  3. Told governments they had a duty to welfare of the community as well as to the property holder.

Potter, David M. *People of Plenty.* Chicago: University of Chicago Press, 1954.
  Potter describes our ways of thinking, living and believing in America as a land of plenty and opportunity in which he shows the influence of this hopeful creed on our politics, on our attitude toward democracy, economic problems, business, and our world outlook.

Prothro, James W. *The Dollar Decade: Business Ideas in the 1920's.* Baton Rouge, Louisiana: Louisiana State University Press, 1954.

Quinn, Theodore K. *Giant Business: Threat to Democracy.* New York: Exposition Press, 1953.
  The story of a self-made, self-educated man who rose to the Vice-Presidency of General Electric, and then on the very threshold of selection as its President resigned his position for ethical reasons.

————. *Giant Corporations: Challenge to Freedom.* New York: Exposition press, 1956.

————. *The Individual in Business Society.* New York: John L. Elliott Institute, 1958.

Rader, Melvin Miller. *Ethics and Society: An Appraisal of Social Ideas.* New York: Henry Holt and Company, 1950.

Radin, Max. "Law and the Dishonest Vendor," *The Lawful Pursuit of Gain.* Boston: Houghton Mifflin, 1931.
  Advertising has to examine its morals. Things have gotten out of hand by allowing advertising to become a business in itself.

————. *Manners and Morals of Business.* New York: The Bobbs-Merrill Company, 1939.
  A psuedo historical approach drawing inferences toward the proposition that "A world without gauchy advertising, without high-pressure salesmen, without economic bribery, without exploitation of labor, without fraud or intrigue in business. . . We should be abundantly satisfied if we could think of it as a remote but not unattainable ideal." Business has made rules for itself and broken them for many years. For a still longer time, political authority has made rules for business and failed to enforce them. And in all cases the rules have had in mind the prevention of those practices which are derived from greed.

Randall, C. B. *A Creed for Free Enterprise*. Boston: Little, Brown and Co., 1952.
    The author's personal feelings on the major categories of business which require ethical decisions.
Randall, John Herman. *The Ethical Challenge of a Pluralistic Society*. New York: New York Society for Ethical Culture, 1959.
Rasmussen, Albert; Taft, Charles P.; and Johnson, Byron L. *Relating Faith to Decision*. New York: Department of the Church and Economic Life, Division of Christian Life and Work, The National Council of Churches of Christ in the U.S.A., 1961.
    A theologian and two Christian laymen discuss the issue of compromise as it relates to the making of difficult decisions in daily work.
Riesman, David. *The Lonely Crowd: A Study of the Changing American Character*. New Haven, Connecticut: Yale University Press, 1950.
    This work is a sophisticated research study of the change in the social character of the "ideal" American from that of "inner-directed" to "other-directed." Such areas as the agents of character formation, political apathy, socialization, the "cult of effortlessness," media and political leaders are analyzed.
Robinson, H. M. *Relativity in Business Morals*. Boston: Houghton Mifflin, 1928.
Ropke, Wilhelm. *A Humane Economy: The Social Framework of the Free Market*. Translated from German. Chicago: Henry Regnery Company, 1960.
    Economics is put in its place in this book. Mr. Ropke looks at Economics from a humanist viewpoint. It is a philosophical treatise on the view of the world today.
Ross, Irwin. *The Image Merchants*. New York: Doubleday and Company, 1959. 271 pages.
    A newsman's rather one-sided report on the questionable practices which characterize the actions of relatively few who call themselves public relations people—harking back more accurately to the press agentry of a past era.
Russell, Bertrand. *Human Society in Ethics and Politics*. London, England: Allen and Unwin, 1954.
Ryerson, Edward L. *A Businessman's Concept of Citizenship*. Privately Printed, 1960.
    A series of lectures delivered by the writer in Australia during the fall of 1958, under the auspices of the Fulbright Committee. An analysis of the responsibility of citizens, and that of the corporations and the community. Some aspects of public relations are also given.
Salvadori, Massimo. *The Economics of Freedom*. New York: Doubleday and Company, 1959.
Schramm, Wilbur. *Responsibility in Mass Communication*. New York: Harper and Brothers, 1957.
Schrodinger, Erwin. *Science and Humanism*. London, England: The Cambridge University Press, 1951.
    Treats science and humanistic behavior patterns as they affect value and moral judgments, and their conflicts.

Schuster, Sir George. *Christianity and Human Relations in Industry*. London, England. The Epworth Press, 1951.

Scott, William G. *The Social Ethic in Management Literature*. Atlanta, Georgia: School of Business Administration, Georgia State College of Business Administration, 1959.

Selekman, Benjamin M. *A Moral Philosophy for Management*. New York: McGraw-Hill Book Company, Inc., 1959.

Points out possible pitfalls in the new posture of moral and social responsibility assumed by business in the past 25 years. Cynicism and self-righteousness at one extreme and the danger of perfectionism and assuming too great a moral burden at the other. Discussion leads to the question of what aspect of morality should be emphasized and implemented by business. "Justice" is suggested as what is desired by the various individuals and groups associated with the enterprise. This requires a type of "constitutionalism"—checks on power to protect rights and interests. This grows out of the negotiation of trade-union agreements—the agreements are types of constitutions. Management confronted with the dilemma of "the technical must versus the ethical ought" is reserved certain powers—allocating resources and scheduling activity. But these powers are subject to rights granted employees and their unions.

Selekman, Sylvia, and Selekman, B. "Human Association as Tamer of Power," *Power and Morality in a Business Society*. New York: McGraw-Hill Book Company, Inc., 1956.

Morality and ethics are an outgrowth of human association. The preoccupation of our generation with moral issues reflects a growing concern with ethical responsibility.

Sharp, Frank, and Fox, Phillip G. *Business Ethics*. New York: Appleton Century Company, Inc., 1937.

The authors conclude that in morality, intent is everything.

Smelser, Neil J. *Social Change in the Industrial Revolution*. Chicago: The University of Chicago Press, 1959. pp. 63–79.

The work is an application of theory to the British Cotton Industry. In this particular portion, he deals with the early stages of structural differentiation with the individual worker in his spinning and allied activities as it was related to the weaver's ethics and religion.

Smethurst, Arthur F. *Modern Science and Christian Beliefs*. London, England: James Nisbet and Company, Ltd., 1955.

A book concerned with the effects of the conflict between Christian beliefs and modern science traced from the seventeenth century scientific revolution up to the present writing.

Smith, James Ward, and Jamison, A. Leland (eds.). *The Shaping of American Religion*. Princeton, New Jersey: Princeton University Press, 1961.

Volume I—A general review of religion in American life.

Volume II—Sometimes a comparison of the church and its relation to and effect upon the economic world may be similar to the fact that depending upon the community, a local clergyman will find his political role spelled out for him. He may alter that role by strength of personality and by other personal attributes he brings to the job, but his constituency sets the basic framework.

Solo, Robert A. (ed.). *Economics and the Public Interest.* New Brunswick, New Jersey: Rutgers University Press, 1955.

Sorokin, Pitirim A., and Lunden, Walter A. *Power and Morality: Who Shall Guard the Guardians?* Boston: P. Sargent, 1959.

Stace, W. T. *Religion and the Modern Mind.* Philadelphia: J. B. Lippincott Company, 1960. (Chapters III, VI, and XI.)

The problem of using "subjective and relative values" to discuss ethical and moral problems is discussed. The concept of value of any type is related to the concept of purpose. Any attempt to destroy a belief in purpose is an attempt to destroy the belief that value is a factor in the universe.

Staley, Eugene (ed.). *Creating an Industrial Civilization.* New York: Harper and Brothers, 1952.

Stern, F. M. *Capitalism in America.* New York: Rinehart and Company, 1951.

Sutherland, Edwin H. *White Collar Crime.* New York: Holt, Rinehart, and Winston, 1949. pp. 1–28, 217–233.

A look at crime in the supposedly less criminal areas of society. Crime in the white collar groups, and in upper levels of society in general is examined. Author challenges old ideas that crime is largely concentrated in lower economic groups. Material presented consists of comprehensive indictment of white collar behavior.

Survey Research Center. *Big Business from the Viewpoint of the Public.* Ann Arbor, Michigan: University of Michigan, 1951.

Sutton, F. K., *et al. The American Business Creed.* Cambridge, Massachusetts: Harvard University Press, 1956.

A penetrating study of the historical philosophies that affected present business traditions and ethical standards.

Taeusch, Carl F. *Policy and Ethics in Business.* New York: McGraw-Hill Book Company, Inc., 1931.

A case method approach to policy and ethics in business. Emphasis on the legality of the problems in each case. Some of the laws and their significance is discussed.

Tarbell, I. M. *The History of the Standard Oil Company.* New York: Mc-Clure, Phillips and Co., 1904.

A complete history of the oil company and the Rockefeller method of management.

Tawney, R. H. *The Acquisitive Society.* New York: Harcourt, Brace, & Howe, 1920.

————. *Religion and the Rise of Capitalism.* New York: Harcourt, Brace and Co., Inc., 1926.

The scope and content of 19th century Christian ethics is undergoing a revision and an attempt is being made to restate the practical implications of the social ethics of the Christian faith, in a form sufficiently comprehensive to provide a standard by which judgment of the collective actions and institutions of mankind can be made.

Thompson, Stewart. *Management Creeds and Philosophies: Top Management Guides in Our Changing Economy.* New York: American Management Association, 1958.

Thorelli, Hans B. *The Federal Antitrust Policy.* Baltimore: The Johns Hopkins Press, 1955.

The author deals with the antitrust policy evolution through the social science interpretation of its origination and institutionalization. A certain form of public policy can be achieved to provide for an optimum condition under which competition may be "workable."

Tillich, Paul. *Dynamics of Faith.* New York: Harper and Brothers, 1957.

An analysis of the changing nature of faith and the differences between faith and belief. Also touches upon the conflicts between faith, as revealed in religion, and belief, as shown in science and scientific thinking.

————. *Love, Power and Justice.* New York: Oxford University Press, 1960.

Tillich discusses the qualities of Love where love is not a matter of intention or demand but a happening or gift; Power whereby spiritual power is assumed to be the greatest and ultimate power; and Justice which is reached only if both the demand for universal law and the demand of the particular situation are accepted and made effective for the concrete situation.

————. *The Protestant Era.* Chicago: University of Chicago Press, 1948. (Chapters VIII, IX and X.)

Analysis of manners in which various systems of philosophy and religion attempt to meet problems of the changing world with ethical implications.

Titmuss, R. H. *The Irresponsible Society.* London, England: Fabian Society, 1960.

Toulmin, H. P., Jr. *Trade Agreements and the Anti-Trust Laws.* Cincinnati: W. H. Anderson and Company. (1946 supplement.)

A detailed analysis of the effects of the anti-trust laws on business transactions and behavior.

Tufts, James H. *America's Social Morality.* New York: Henry Holt and Co., 1933.

Vivas, Eliseo. *The Moral Life and the Ethical Life.* Chicago, Illinois: The University of Chicago Press, 1950.

A book on the differences between the moral life as based on social standards and criteria and the ethical life as based on Christian ethics.

Von Hildebrand, Dietrich. *Christian Ethics.* New York: David McKay Company, Inc. 1953.

A thorough analysis and explanation of Christian ethics as expressed in the ultimate value of love of God and neighbor.

Wallach, Henry C. *The Cost of Freedom: A New Look at Capitalism.* New York: Harper and Brothers, 1960.

Wallis, Louis. *Sociological Study of the Bible.* Chicago: University of Chicago Press, 1912.

This evolutionary study of Christendom, in the form of research into ancient history, points out that the vital religious ideas of Christian society took shape in response to social forces.

Walton, Clarence C. "Ethical Theory, Society Expectations, and Marketing Practices," *Social Responsibilities of Marketing,* William Stevens, editor. Proceedings of the Winter Conference, American Marketing Association. New York: American Marketing Association, 1962.
   The ethical problems relating to marketing, especially marketing practices, i.e., advertising, are discussed and an attempt is made to justify them.
Ward, Dudley. *The American Economy—Attitude and Opinions.* New York: Harper and Brothers, 1955.
————. *Goals of Economic Life.* New York: Harper and Brothers, 1953.
————. *The Social Creed of the Methodist Church,* New York: Abingdon Press, 1961.
   The latest (1960) version of the creed of the Methodist Church provides a Christian mandate on the widest range of issues inherent in the nuclear-space age with its rapid social change.
Weber, Max. *The Protestant Ethic and the Spirit of Capitalism.* New York: Oxford University Press, 1958.
   The "Weber thesis" is basically connecting ascetic protestantism and capitalistic economic development. The essence of this thesis is that this value-system is a particularly fruitful breeding ground for a social structure and for individual motivation which encourage the development of bourgeoise capitalist institutions.
Whyte, William H., Jr. *The Organization Man.* Garden City, New York: Doubleday and Co., 1957.
   Traces the growth of the organization man ideology and its practical effects. The main influences on the formation of this ideology are the decline of the Protestant Ethic, the rise of the Social Ethic, belief in scientism, and emphasis on belongingness and togetherness.
Widgerly, Alban G. *Christian Ethics in History and Modern Life.* New York: Round Table Press, Inc., 1940.
   A scholarly presentation of Christian ethics with consideration of its implications for modern life. An historical background is introduced to show the nature and detail of ethics from classical examples and presentations in Christian history.
Wiener, Norbert. *The Human Use of Human Beings.* New York: Doubleday and Company., Inc., 1954.
   This book is devoted to the impact of the Gibbsian (U.S. physicist) point of view on modern life, both through substantive changes it has made in working science, and through the changes it has made indirectly in our attitude to life in general. It contains an element of technical description as well as philosophical component which concerns what we do and how we should react to the new world that confronts us. "Cybernetics" thus deals with the larger theory of message sas a probabilistic theory. Society can only be understood through a study of such messages and their communications facilities.
Wilcox, Clair. *Public Policies Toward Business.* Homewood, Illinois: Richard D. Irwin, 1955.
Wilcox, Walter M. *Social Responsibility in Farm Leadership.* New York: Harper and Brothers, 1960.

Williams, Raymond. *The Long Revolution*. New York: Columbia University Press, 1961.

The "long revolution" refers to the democratic, industrial, and cultural revolutions transforming our society. Inquiry is made into these changes and their impact on the individual. Considered are three aspects of culture: questions in the theory of culture, historical analysis of certain cultural institutions and forms, and problems of meaning and action in the contemporary cultural situation. The significance of the "creative idea" is examined and creativity is proposed as a possible key concept in discussion of contemporary culture. The cultural traditions of a nation are related to the society which developed it and the complex relationship between the individual and society are analyzed. Indicated is a necessary strength: against arbitrary power, against all conscious confusion and weakening of human effort.

Williams, Robin M., Jr. *American Society*. New York: Alfred A. Knopf, 1960.

Worthy, James C. *Big Business and Free Man*. New York: Harper and Brothers, 1959.

Wylie, Philip, *Generation of Vipers*. New York: Farrar and Rinehart, Inc., 1942. (Chapter 10.)

The author cites the very low level of business morality in the early 40's and states that any procedure that was technically legal, became the businessman's definition of ethics and the public definition of morality.

PERIODICALS

Abrams, F. W. "Management's Responsibilities in a Complex World," *Harvard Business Review*, Vol. XXIX, May 1951, pp. 29-34.

Agnew, Cornelius R. Jr. "Putting Board Members to Work," *Public Relations Journal*, Vol. 16, December 1960, pp. 24-26.

In name of good community relations, companies are called upon to encourage participation of executives on boards of community agencies, with a call upon agencies to make the experience fruitful for both the institution and participant.

Allen, R. N. "Leadership to Maintain Free Enterprise," *Controller*, Vol. XXVII, July 1959, pp. 320-322.

Apel, Hans. "Should We Shorten the Work Week?" *Challenge*, Vol. 10, March 1962, pp. 320-31.

Noting that as result of all past technological revolutions, the work week was shortened, this economist feels the same must be done gradually, to avoid a permanent unemployment problem as result of automation today.

"Are Business Ethics Slipping?" *Purchasing*, Vol. 45, September 1, 1958, pp. 15-16.

A survey of purchasing agents in regard to current thought on the matter of business ethics. Some of the information obtained is: have ethics improved or declined; are there ethical differences between business and government; opinion on business gifts; and practicality of a code of ethics.

Austin, Robert W. "Code of Conduct for Executives," *Harvard Business Review*, Vol. 39, September–October, 1961, p. 53.

A code of conduct is proposed by the author affirming the fact that business managers have overriding obligations to others and that they have a duty to reveal the facts where their personal interests are involved. In contrast to laws and corporate policies, this proposed code would be an internal incentive to sound decision making.

Barnard, Chester I. "Elementary Conditions of Business Morals," *California Management Review*, Vol. I, Fall, 1958, pp. 1-13.

Batten, H. A. "Why I Believe Good Morals are Good Business," *Printers Ink*, October 19, 1951, pp. 43-45.

A brief article discussing unethical practices and pointing up the case of the exam cheaters at West Point. He then goes on to say that we can handle or assume ethical practices so long as we do not excuse them; we can enforce ethical practices by the generation of ideas.

Baum, M. "Case for Business Civilization," *Harvard Business Review*, Vol. XXXVIII, November 1960, pp. 56-64.

A discussion of the indictment against American business, including the charges that the business culture causes drastic damage to individual character and conduct; and that the business culture debases our professional and political behavior by its complete disregard for the social and cultural consequences of business decisions.

Baumhart, Raymond C. "How Ethical are Businessmen?" *Harvard Business Review*, Vol. 39, No. 4, July–August, 1961, p. 6.

Business executives show a strong desire to improve business behavior, as they discuss frankly the wrongdoing in the business community, and sketch a serious problem for the future: things can't improve unless top management stands its ground and makes it clear that ethical methods are the only approved way of doing business.

Berle, Adolph A., Jr., "For Whom Corporate Managers are Trustees," *Harvard Law Review*, Vol. XXXXV, June 1932.

Black, J. M. "Changing Image of American Management," *Harvard Business Review*, Vol. 38, No. 3, May–June, 1960, pp. 4-8.

A study of the present image of business management and discussion of the history and the trend of the management image.

Blum, Albert A. "Collective Bargaining, Ritual or Reality," *Harvard Business Review*, November–December 1961, pp. 63-69.

The author discusses fallacies of bargaining and the need for more cooperation to prevent government intervention. If the present system is to be maintained, higher ethical standards must be developed in the relationship between these two groups.

Blum, Fred H. "Social Audit of the Enterprise," *Harvard Business Review*, Vol. 36, March–April, 1958, pp. 77-86.

A description of and support for the "social audit" of the business—a yearly appraisal of how the firm is meeting its social responsibilities, with the accent on worker job satisfaction.

Boulding, Kenneth. "Religious Foundations of Economic Progress," *Harvard Business Review*, Vol. 30, May 1952, pp. 33-40.

Religion is important because it helps man decide if he wants the right things. That is why the Protestant Ethic is important.

Bowen, H. R. "Business Management: A Profession?" *Annals of the American Academy of Political and Social Science*, Vol. CCLXXXXVII, January 1955, pp. 112-119.

————. "How Public Spirited is American Business?" *Annals of the American Academy of Political and Social Science*, Vol. CCLXXX, March 1952, pp. 82-89.

"Bread, Freedom, and Businessmen," *Fortune*, September 1951.

Brown, Ray E. "6 Executive Bad Habits—and How to Break Them." *Office Management and American Business*, June 1960.

Many executives compound their difficulties by falling into the bad habits of 1) A policy of first-come-first-served, 2) Unpredictability, 3) Impulse, 4) Susceptibility of flattery, 5) Over expansiveness, and 6) Lack of self control. Main problem is to recognize deviations. Avoid fatigue and observe other good health practices.

Bullis, H. A. "Businessman's Social Responsibilities," *Commercial and Financial Chronicle*, Vol. CLXXXI, May 5, 1955, p. 2079.

————. "Road to Business Leadership: Humanity, Productivity, Ownership, Understanding," *Management Review*, Vol. XXXIX, June 1950, pp. 302-304.

Burnham, James. "The Suicidal Mania of American Business," *Partisan Review*, January 1950, pp. 47-63.

"Business Ethics," *New Republic*, Vol. 140, February 2, 1959, p. 2.

"Business Ethics—Too Much Grey Area," *Fortune*, Vol. 62, September 1960, pp. 127-128.

An editorial that points up how few businesses have a stated code of conduct but rather that business relies on the individual ethics of their executives. The editorial fosters the idea of an informed conscience; a combination of mental and moral energy.

"The Business Inquisition," *Sales Management*, Vol. 86, May 19, 1961, pp. 35-40.

An article urging business to take steps to remove questionable practices before the government steps in to do it for them.

"Business is Still in Trouble," *Fortune*, May 1949, pp. 67-71, 196-200.

A majority of people still think business is too greedy and that it has played a large part in keeping prices too high. They think government should keep a sharp eye on business. Public relations will not suffice—good business public relations is good performance, publicly appreciated.

Buzby, G. C., President, Chilton Company. "Policies—A Guide to What a Company Stands For," *Management Record*, Vol. 24, No. 3, March 1962.

Executives' practical problems—communication of policies (moral and ethical principles) and getting everyone to act and live in accordance with them.

Campbell, Thomas C. "Capitalism and Christianity," *Harvard Business Review*, July-August, 1957, pp. 37-44.

Businessmen wonder whether or not capitalism and Christianity are compatible philosophies. They believe that no guidelines are presented by Christianity. Campbell believes agreement is possible and lists four basic goals which are stressed in religion as well as our economic system.

Canham, Erwin D. "The Value of Self-Criticism," *Vital Speeches*, Vol. 26, December 1959, p. 147.

―――――. "World, National Outlook, and the Role of Businessmen," *Commercial and Financial Chronicle*, Vol. CLXXXX, October 1959, pp. 1594-1595.

"Cash Value of Ideas." *New Republic*, 141, November 16, 1959. p. 5.

American society is on the downgrade. Unfortunately, the bribe and the illegal payment have become commonplace, and this example has been set by our leaders.

Cavers, David F. "Antitrust: Symbol into Problem," *Fortune*, July 1949.

Successive government legal victories have converted U.S. antitrust laws from a mere symbol of economic democracy into a general economic problem. In 1937 Professor Thurman Arnold called those laws the expression "of a society which unconsciously felt the need of great organizations," yet excluded them from "moral and logical ideology." Enforcement was "a pure ritual." (Enforcement of the antitrust laws is no longer a ritual, but many of its consequences remain an economic mystery). This article traces the problem's history and indicates main current aspects.

Chamberlin, Neil. "What is Management's Right to Manage?" *Fortune*, July 1949, pp. 68-70.

At the root of the problem of management's right to manage is the increasing insubstantiality of management's ability to maintain it. People can be managed and directed only with their own consent. Cooperation, without which the property right is reduced to a power of disposition, cannot be commanded. The property right of the stockholders, exercised for them by management, can be made meaningful only with the cooperation of all those who are actually needed to operate the business, including the workers. The management prerogative is the power to make decisions and to see their effectuation within whatever framework of discretion may exist. Collective bargaining is in fact one method of management—a process for making business decisions that can be carried out.

Chamberlin, William H. "Christianity and Capitalism," *Wall Street Journal*, April 16, 1948.

The author answers the criticisms of the Christian Churches and rejects their socialist-slanted recommendation and counters with a recommendation calling for mutual understanding and co-existence.

Chapple, E. D. "New Role for Executives: Dramatic Shift in Business Civilization," *Nation's Business*, Vol. XXXXVII, May 1959, pp. 58-60.

"The Churches Speak to Business," *Fortune*, Vol. 38, December 1948, pp. 122-131.

The Christian Churches criticize the capitalistic system of business for the inequalities that it produces and advocates that the control of business activity should be placed in the hands of the government.

Clark, John M. "The Changing Basis of Economic Responsibility," *Journal of Political Economy*, March 1916.

Cochran, T. C. "Business and the Democratic Tradition," *Harvard Business Review*, Vol. 34, March–April, 1956, pp. 39-48.

The author maintains that to hope for moral or spiritual inspiration from any business enterprise is asking for new functions from an institution that is designed to supply material goods. However, he cites that the modern corporation has become more than an economic institution and its managers now have more than a material responsibility.

Cole, A. H. "Evolving Perspective of Businessmen," *Harvard Business Review*, Vol. XXVII, June 1949, pp. 123-128.

————. "Transcendental Aspects of Business," *Harvard Business Review*, Vol. 36, No. 3, 1958, p. 51.

Ethical and moral implications in relation to business; and the direction into which it has proceeded up to present time. A fresh attitude is required to solve some of the problems.

Coleman, J. S. "Aiming Toward a Workable Society," *Office Executive*, Vol. XXXIII, April 1958, pp. 9-11.

————. "New Dimensions in Business," *Commercial and Financial Chronicle*, Vol. CLXXXV, January 17, 1957, pp. 222-223.

The necessity of American businessmen to transcend from exclusive interest in their respective positions in industry to undertaking as well a constructive role in developing and supporting domestic and internal policies is discussed.

Collier, A. T. "Business Leadership and a Creative Society," *Harvard Business Review*, Vol. 31, January 1953, pp. 29-38.

It is the responsibility of the business leader to help the worker increase his usefulness and creativeness as well as achieving his individuality. This it a difficult challenge but one which must be met.

————. "Debate at Wickersham Mills," *Harvard Business Review*, Vol. 38, May–June, 1960, pp. 49-63.

A dialogue of a company board meeting at which the candidates for firm president present their qualifications for the top job; ethical implications are found in what the respective aspirants hope to accomplish for the company and themselves.

————. "Faith in a Creative Society," *Harvard Business Review*, Vol. XXXV, May 1957, pp. 35-41.

————. "Social Responsibilities of the Businessman," *Management Review*, XXXXVI, July 1957, pp. 62-70.

When businessmen engage in activities outside of their businesses (charitable and civic), what are the limits on his time, how should he discharge his duty? The article points out the duty of businessmen to the community and government but leaves the decision up to the individual.

Colton, Raymond R. "A Code for Industrial Purchasing," *Advanced Management*, April 1961, pp. 20-22.

The purchasing department is an integral part of a business structure, carrying out varied and numerous functions of major importance. In his business dealings, loyalty, justice, faith, and common decency are of prime importance to the purchasing agent.

Cordiner, R. J. "Corporate Citizenship and the Businessman: A Working Program for Action," *Management Record,* Vol. XXXXVIII, July 1959, pp. 15-19.

————. "New Dimension in Business Leadership," *Saturday Review,* Vol. XXXXI, January 18, 1958, pp. 30-32.

"Corporate Directors and Business Ethics," *Business Record,* September 1961, pp. 31-49.

A survey of some techniques used by directors to ensure ethical practices within a business. The best method for providing for ethical practices is to employ officials of "proven honesty and integrity." Some of the techniques employed are policy statements, questionnaires, and audits. Examples of some are given.

"Corporate Morality and Personal Morality," *Christian Century,* Vol. 78, February 22, 1961, p. 228.

The author decries the separation of personal acts and business decisions. He concludes that America should be worried about free enterprise in the light of recent ethical problems.

Craig, C. F. "Business Ideal and Community Progress," *Public Utilities Fortnightly,* Vol. LVII, March 29, 1956, pp. 480-482.

"Crisis in Business Ethics," *Purchasing,* Vol. 45. September 1, 1958, pp. 53, 55-57.

A strong stand deriding the apparent influx of salesmen's attempts to use gift-giving or stronger persuasive measures to influence purchasing agents.

Culliton, James W. "Business and Religion," *Harvard Business Review,* January–February, 1949, pp. 265-271.

Culliton presents a discussion of the interrelation of business and spiritual values, and a recommendation for greater application of Christian religion to business.

Daiute, R. J. "Mary Parker Follett: Philosopher of Business," *Advanced Management,* July-August, 1961, p. 18.

Miss Follett's life pointed up one important thing: look at things simply.

Dale, Ernest. "Management Must Be Made Accountable," *Harvard Business Review,* Vol. 38, March–April, 1960, pp. 49-59.

A proposal for various types review boards which can serve as voluntary control groups to offset the state of unaccountability which the managerial class enjoys today.

Davenport, John. "In the Midst of Plenty," *Fortune,* Vol. 63, April 1961. pp. 101, 106-109.

Today's businessman has an ethical duty to think of the poor and unfortunate. The author shows that although poverty has been with us in the past, it need not be in the future.

Davenport, Russell W. "The Greatest Opportunity on Earth," *Fortune,* October 1949.

David, Donald K. "Business Responsibilities in an Uncertain World," *Harvard Business Review* (Supplement), May 1949.

Davis, Keith. "Can Business Afford to Ignore Social Responsibilities?" *California Management Review,* Vol. II, Spring, 1960, pp. 70-76.

Davis, Ralph C. "Frederick W. Taylor and the American Philosophy of Management," *Advanced Management*, December 1959, pp. 4-7.

The impact of F. W. Taylor on American Management is discussed. Taylor believed that scientific management supplied a basis for a sound business philosophy. Davis suggests that if "scientific management" were understood it would have a powerful impact on legislation as well as corporate policy.

————. "A Philosophy of Management," *Advanced Management,* Vol. XXIV, April 1959, pp. 5-6.

Davis expresses what he feels are the 10 requirements for a sound philosophy of management to operate in a free enterprise economy. He speaks briefly of moral development and sound business relations as embodied in a moral philosophy of ethical principles.

Demos, R. "The American Image of Success," *Harvard Business Review,* Vol. 39, March–April, 1961, pp. 45-50.

This is an intelligent and philosophical inquiry into the nature of success. The problem arises when the image of success is projected into areas where it is not relevant.

————. "Business and the Good Society," *Harvard Business Review,* Vol. XXXIII, July 1955, pp. 33-44.

Dempsey, B. W. "Roots of Business Responsibility," *Harvard Business Review,* July 1949, pp. 393-404.

DeVoto, Bernard. "Why Professors are Suspicious of Business," *Fortune,* Vol. XXXXIII, April 1951, pp. 114-115.

A professor who feels that he has been too often either insulted or short-changed by business, blaming this distrust on skepticism of business intelligence as it is manifested. The principal begetter of distrust is sighted as the advertising agency.

Doan, L. I. "Fundamental Role of Business Is to Operate Profitably," *Commercial and Financial Chronicle,* Vol. CLXXXVI, July 18, 1957, p. 286.

Dodd, E. Merrick, Jr. "For Whom Are Corporate Managers Trustees?" *Harvard Law Review,* Vol. XXXXV, May 8, 1932, pp. 1145-1163.

Drucker, Peter F. "Big Business and the National Purpose," *Harvard Business Review,* Vol. 40, No. 2, March–April, 1962, pp. 49-59.

This article presents new areas of business responsibilities including: maintaining America's position in the world market; innovating policies; identifying the firm with the public interest; developing a code of conduct to further human values and serve the national purpose.

Duddy, E. A. "The Moral Implications of Business as a Profession," *Journal of Business,* April 1945, pp. 72-73.

Eells, Richard. "Social Responsibility, Can Business Survive the Change?" *Business Horizons,* Winter, 1959, pp. 33-41.

Management has the task of restructuring the corporation theory to integrate debatable social responsibilities into a rational view of business operations, not too far removed from established premises of corporate practice.

Eppert, Ray R. "Moral Basis for Business Leadership," *Management Record,* Vol. 24, No. 3, March 1962.

Morals of the corporation can be nothing more than the sum total of the moral behavior of the individual persons in the organization. Corporate policy is carried out by the individual members of management. Corporate morals work from the top down, not from the bottom up. It is difficult to censure subordinates who are taking their cues from their superiors, and this is a chain reaction which leads right up to and into the presidential office.

Ericson, R. F. "Looking Around," *Harvard Business Review,* Vol. 36 No. 3, 1958, p. 143.

Article discusses management's responsibility to society in the light of an ideal nature of business philosophy. Author feels that reeducation of management may be the answer to moral problems facing business society.

————. "Should Management Be Idealistic?" *Harvard Business Review,* September 1958, pp. 143-144.

If management does not voluntarily demonstrate an awareness of the importance of an adequate synthesis of non-economic and economic factors in its decision making, other blocks, unions and government will eventually seek to compel such attention.

"Ethics in the Market Place," *America,* Vol. 100, March 7, 1959, pp. 651-2.

"Ethics of the Professions and of Business," *Annals of the American Academy of Political and Social Science,* Vol. 101, 1922.

This issue is devoted to a discussion of ethics of the time and several examples of business codes are included.

Finklestein, Louis. "The Businessman's Moral Failure," *Fortune,* September 1958, pp. 116-117.

Rabbi Finklestein believes that if businessmen fail to assume their moral obligations it will be the "American Tragedy." The practical value of ethical practices and suggested methods for installing them are discussed.

Finn, David. "Struggle for Ethics in Public Relations," *Harvard Business Review,* January–February, 1959.

The issue is to what extent should business respect the basic principles of the democratic process and the right of the people to make up their own minds, rather than attempt to engineer consent through whatever techniques seem to work. Conclusion is that there is no clear-cut answer, but that management should discuss it in order to determine the ethical threshold of its public relations activity.

Fisher, William, Jr. "Social Agencies: A New Challenge for Public Relations," *The Quarterly Review of Public Relations,* Vol. 4, April 1959, pp. 14-23.

As a proposal for worthwhile community relations activity, business public relations practitioners are called upon to help the much-misunderstood social service agencies to better interpret their vital services.

Flanders, Ralph E. "Economics Collides with Ethics," *American Economic Review* (Supplement), May 1948, pp. 357-467.

Fleming, E. D. "Manners and Morals in Business," *Cosmopolitan,* Vol. CXXXXVI, March 1959, pp. 24-81.

Ford, Henry II. "Business Ethics in 1961," *Vital Speeches,* May 15, 1961, p. 454.

Either the businessman will straighten up his ethical practices or some "unfriendly" persons will do the task.

Frederick, William C. "The Growing Concern Over Business Responsibility," *California Management Review* Vol. II, Summer, 1960.

Furash, Edward E. "What Businessmen Think of Industrial Espionage," *Harvard Business Review,* November-December, 1959.

Discusses quantitative findings in Harvard Business Review Study based on 1558 complete questionnaires—a 21 per cent return. Results indicate the frequency of industrial spying and secret stealing in American business is quite low.

Gellerman, Saul W. "The Ethics of Personality Testing," *Personnel,* November–December, 1958, pp. 30-35.

The invasion of the inner person by psychological testing is discussed in relation to its use in business. The author feels that unless test users develop a code of ethics and can assure a testee that the results will remain confidential, personality testing will lost its effectiveness to companies.

"Giving More Public Service," *Steel,* May 18, 1959, pp. 99-106.

Goldschmidt, Walter. "Ethics and the Structure of Society: An Ethnological Contribution to the Sociology of Knowledge," *American Anthropologist,* Vol. 53, No. 4, October–December, 1951, pp. 507-524.

Goldschmidt describes the position of the individual within a capitalist structure of society such as the Northwest California ethics which placed the focus of more responsibility upon the individual, a moral responsibility and a moral demand which produced a pattern of individual guilt and the concept of sin.

Gras, N.S.B. "Capitalism—Concepts and History," *Bulletin of the Business History Society,* Vol. XVI, April 1942, pp. 21-34.

————. "Leadership Past and Present," *Harvard Business Review,* July 1949, pp. 419-437.

Graves, W. Brooks. "Codes of Ethics for Business and Commercial Organization," *The International Journal of Ethics,* Vol. XXXV, October 1924.

Halper, John B. "Public Affairs—Management's Fastest Growing Relation," *The Quarterly Review of Public Relations,* Vol. 5, January 1960, pp. 23-29.

A strong case for management's employment of a special staff to administer the enterprise's participation in the growing-need area of public affairs.

Hamilton, Walton. "Affectation with Public Interest," *Yale Law Review,* 1930, pp. 1089-1112.

Handlin, Oscar and Handlin, Mary F. "Origins of the American Business Corporation," *Journal of Economic History,* Vol. V, May 1945, pp. 1-23.

The article describes the process by which the business corporation has acquired its modern character. Development of the economic ideas began centuries ago, but in Massachusetts the corporate charter took on new interpretations (as contrasted to Europe) because of the American democratic concepts.

Hartman, Robert S. "Does a Corporation Need Spiritual Objectives?" *Nationwide World,* Vol. 3, July–August, 1961, pp. 9-10.

A theistic declaration that corporations must have spiritual objectives in order to be able to take into account the human nature of people in its dealing with employees.

"Have Corporations a Higher Duty than Profits?" *Fortune,* Vol. LXII, August 1960, pp. 108-109.

An exploration of two theories, one, that management do justice to the stockholders and two, that management be guided by long-term profits. Fortune suggests the second alternative and proceeds to point out how this will obviate the need for the first theory.

Hay, R. D. "A Proposed Code of Ethics for Business Administration Educators," *Advanced Management,* September 1961, pp. 22-23.

A good, concise article that outlines the college professor's responsibility to the student, parent, community, profession, and to the school administration.

Hayes, A. J. "Labor's Fight to Clean House," *Management Record,* July 1957, pp. 245-6.

The responsibility to establish ethical standards for labor is labor's. This article tells briefly what the unions are doing for themselves.

————. "Maintaining the Values of a Free Society," *Vital Speeches,* Vol. XXIV, April 1, 1958, pp. 374-377.

Heald, Morrell. "Management's Responsibility to Society: The Growth of the Idea," *Business History Review,* Vol. XXXI, Winter, 1957, pp. 375-84.

Even in the laissez-faire days there was a "corporate conscience," well-defined and with active manifestations. A prominent aspect of the new capitalism is the emergence of a new "corporate conscience," a recognition on the part of management of an obligation to the society it serves, not only for maximum economic performance but for humane and constructive social policies as well.

Helleiner, K. F. "Moral Conditions of Economic Growth," *Journal of Economic History,* Vol. XI, Spring, 1951, pp. 97-106.

Paper presents factors in operation (ascetic Christianity) in Western society to repress wealth-getting. Fraudulent acquisition of wealth was opposed by secular as well as ecclesiastical authorities. The elimination of bad practices has led to secular economic growth.

Henderson, Leon. "Vital Issues Facing Business Today," *Commercial and Financial Chronicle,* August 1, 1946.

Heron, Alexander R. "How Responsible Can Management Be?" *Advanced Management,* Vol. 19, November 1954, pp. 6-9.

The greatest ethical responsibility of management is seen as creating and maintaining full employment by being creative in its business operations.

"The Hidden Trap in Automation," *Dun's Review,* May 1961, p. 53.

The biggest problem with automation is retraining the technologically displaced.

Higgins, Thomas G. "Ethics for Today's Business Society, *The Controller,* Vol. 20, April 1961, pp. 192-6.

These excerpts from a speech indicate that strong character standing up for right may hasten the development of ethics in business.

————. "Morals and Economic Life," *Social Order,* Vol. 10, September 1960, pp. 304-17.
The author feels that although the United States capitalistic system is the most ethical in today's world, American business still needs a widely-accepted moral code.

"A history of American Industry," *Fortune,* following issues:
May 1961, Volume LXIII, No. 5, pp. 129-36, 166, 171, 172, 173.
June 1961, Volume LXIII, No. 6, pp. 165-68, 249-50, 254, 256.
September 1961, Volume LXIV, No. 3, pp. 135-39, 140, 144, 146, 151-52, 156.
October 1961, Volume LXIV, No. 4, pp. 149-52, 170, 175, 176, 180, 182, 185.
November 1961, Volume LXIV, No. 5, pp. 155-58 188, 191, 192, 194, 199.
A review of American business and industry from its beginning in the European industrial revolution through the modern day including the thinking of Beecher, Conwell, Ford, May, Tawney, and the modern authorities in the field.

"The History and Need of American Business Ethics," *Fortune,* Vol. XL, December 1949, pp. 114-158.

Houser, T. V. "Code for Corporate Citizens," *Business Week,* May 18, 1957. p. 97.
Houser touched briefly on executive salaries (set by the marketplace) and then launched into a detailed discussion of the corporation's responsibilities to the employees, stockholders, community, government, and business abroad.

"Industry Claims House is Clean," *Business Week,* December 5, 1959, pp. 28-29.
An examination on the part of executives of ethical standards in the area of operations. Report that relative standards are high and improving.

"Is There a Decline in U.S. Morals?" *U.S. News & World Report,* May 21, 1962, pp. 60-64.
An interview with Dr. Liston Pope, Dean of Yale Divinity School. Dr. Pope discusses such subjects as the diminishing impact of religion in America, the continuing high rate of family breakup, and that right and wrong depend largely on what one has been taught.

Isaacs, H. C. "Managerial Revolution," *Saturday Review,* Vol. XLI, January 18, 1958.

Jasinski, Frank J. "Adapting Organization to New Technology," *Harvard Business Review,* Vol. 37, January-February, 1959, pp. 79-86.
A strong case is presented for making the process of adapting to new technology more than merely one of extending the existing organization—rather a complete appraisal of personnel adjustments as they relate to the changing enterprise must be studied, the author believes.

Jeannings, E. E. "Make Way for the Business Moralist," *Nation's Business,* Vol. XLVII, September 1959.

Johnson, C. D. "Spiritual Responsibility of American Business and Industry," *Vital Speeches,* Vol. XXII, December 15, 1956, pp. 151-153.

Johnson, Harold L. "Business Now Tied to the Public Interest," *Weekly Underwriter,* Vol. CLXXV, December 15, 1956.

————. "Can Businessmen Apply Christianity?" *Harvard Business Review,* September-October, 1957, pp. 68-76.

Basic concepts of Christianity and their usefulness to the businessman are discussed.

————. "Emerging Patterns of Corporate Citizenship," *Vital Speeches,* Vol. XXIV, February 15, 1958, pp. 285-288.

————. "An Evaluation of the Social Responsibility of Business Concept," *Atlantic Economic Review,* Vol. VII, April 1957, pp. 1-5.

Jonassen, Christen T. "The Protestant Ethic and the Spirit of Capitalism in Norway,"*American Sociological Review,* Vol. 12, No. 6, December 1947, pp. 676-686.

Jonassen discusses what Max Weber really said in "The Protestant Ethic and the Spirit of Capitalism," as applied to the Protestant country of Norway.

Jones, Jenkin Lloyd. "American Morals: A Critical Report That is Snowballing," a reprint of a speech, *U.S. News & World Report,* Vol. LII, No. 22, May 28, 1962, pp. 90-93.

A "warning that Americans must arouse themselves to the mediocrity of schools, the trash that poses as literature, the relief system. Mr. Jones wants to know "who is tampering with the soul of America."

He admits the newspapers, (an editor himself) have been in part responsible, and asks that we all look to the hills.

Kaplan, A. D. and Kahn, A. E. "Big Business in a Competitive Society," *Fortune,* (Supplement) Vol. XLVII, February 1953.

"Keeping a High Shine on Ethics," *Business Week,* March 25, 1961, pp. 81-88.

Several methods employed by large corporations to raise or maintain ethical standards are discussed. These cover such areas as policies, conferences and questionnaires to develop or apply standards.

Kensington, C. E. "Moral Responsibilities for Industry," *Personnel Management,* Vol. XLI, June 1959, pp. 63-65.

Kepler, Edwin C. "The New Scope of Community Relations," *The Quarterly Review of Public Relations,* Vol. 6, Winter, 1961, pp. 23-30.

A plea to advance beyond "passive activities" in community relations programs by inaugurating projects which help the community to improve its business climate.

Kerr, Clark. "What Became of the Independent Spirit?" *Fortune,* Vol. XLVIII, July 1953.

Knight, Frank. "Economists and Economic Ethics," *Ethics,* Vol. XLVIII, October 1957.

Kratz, Lawrence A. "The Motivation of the Business Manager," *Behavioral Science,* Vol. 5, No. 4, October 1960, pp. 313-316.

This study concerns itself with what factors the owners of business firms—whether they are individual owners or corporate stockholders—take into account in selecting a business manager to produce the kind of company they are interested in having. Results show, contrary to previous economic theories based on profit maximization, that depending on how closely the owners are involved with the firm, methods of compensation to a manger and his internal motivations are deciding factors in a firm's success.

Lavengood, Lawrence G. "American Business and the Piety of Profits," *Harvard Business Review*, Vol. 37, November-December, 1959, pp. 47-55.
A contention that business gets strongly criticized for the country's troubles, not because it hasn't done its job, but because it implies that it can deliver more than is possible.

Lawrence, D. "Code of Codes," *U.S. News and World Report*, Vol. XXVII, December 28, 1959.

Learned, E. P., Dooly, A. R., and Katz, R. L. "Personal Values and Business Decisions," *Harvard Business Review*, March 1959, pp. 111-120.
An enlightened article on the problem of adapting your personal values to the morals of the society and how to build up guides to action. Good and clear approach of the problem of ethics and business.

Lenhart, R. F., and Schriftgiesser, K. "Management in Politics." *Annals of the American Academy of Political and Social Science*, Vol. CCCXIX, September 1958, pp. 32-40.

Levitt, T. "Dangers of Social Responsibility," *Harvard Business Review*, Vol. XXXVI, September 1958. pp. 41-50.
Business should return to its dominant objection—long-run profit maximization, disregarding the distractions and bureaucracies of government. Virtues such as altruism, self-denial, and charity are alien to competitive economies, according to the author.

Littlejohn, E. "Heirs of the Robber Barons: Changing Face of America," *Vital Speeches*, Vol. XXIV, April 15, 1958, pp. 409-416.

Lubar, Robert. "The Prime Movers," *Fortune*, Vol. 61, February 1960, pp. 98-100, 248.
A descriptive pat-on-the-back to the business leaders who are in the forefront of all of New York City's civic improvement projects.

MacIver, Robert M. "The Social Significance of Professional Ethics," *Annals of the American Academy of Political and Social Science*, January 1955.

"Management in Transition," *Steel*, Vol. CXLV, October 12, 1959, pp. 101-108.

"Manufacturer's Representatives: Saints or Sinners?" *Dun's Review*, May 1962, pp. 67-74.
Article showing the ever increasing need from small business for the services of the manufacturer's representatives, and how at the same time, the larger corporations have also turned to the services of the manufacturer's representatives. The article points up the difficulty of not selling competitive products and the ethics of the representatives.

Mason, Alpheus T. "The Apologetics of Managerialism," *Journal of Business*, Vol. 31, January 1958, pp. 1-11.
Society has passed from the period of owner controlled business to manager controlled firms. It is up to management to help formulate a new ideology to accompany this change.

————. "Business Organized as Power: The New Imperium in Imperio," *American Political Science Review*, Vol. XLIV, June 1950, pp. 323-342.

————. "Welfare Capitalism: Opportunity or Delusion," *Virginia Quarterly Review*, Autumn, 1950, pp. 530-543.

Masse, B. L. "Role of the Christian Employer," *America*, Vol. 98, October 12, 1957, p. 37.

McAdoo, Richard B. "Sabbaticals for Businessmen," *Harper's*, Vol. 224 (1344), May 1962, p. 39.

Just as college professors get a leave of absence periodically, so the author suggests should businessmen. He believes a sabbatical every eleventh year would work out nicely for the businessman. It would give him a broad view of the business world. This is a very interesting appeal and might very well help improve the moral business climate.

McCarthy, J. J. "Keystone of Management: Religion in Business," *Vital Speeches*, Vol. XXIV, March 1, 1958, pp. 303-310.

McGrath, William L. "Political Responsibilities of the U.S. Businessman," *Advanced Management*, August 1959, pp. 6-8.

Businessmen are concerned with political activity which threatens them but don't know how to react. McGrath suggests that they should begin "right at home" to work in politics.

Megginson, Leon C. "Ethical Standards of Conduct in Business," *Advanced Management*, May 1960, pp. 21-23.

The manager has the primary responsibility of being a good steward of the rights of the owners of the business, for they comprise the group that hires him. It is the manager's responsibility to settle the differences between the conflicting interests of customers, suppliers, labor, etc., and maintain balance in the business organization.

Mellon, Richard K. "The Responsibility of Management," *Michigan Business Review*, Vol. VI, May 1954.

Miles, Stephen B., Jr. "Management Politician," *Harvard Business Review*, January-February, Vol. 39, No. 1, 1961, pp. 99-104.

The purposes of business have been shifting, with a greater emphasis today on the social responsibility of corporations. The large-scale corporation has set a pattern for modern day living, states the author, with a greater welfare and social consciousness.

Miller, H. B. "Is Business Meeting Its Obligation to the Public?" *Public Relations Journal*, Vol. 18, May 1962.

A critical blast at some of today's questionable business practices, with an appeal to include the public relations staff in more high-level decision-making to help offset some of the abuses.

Miller, S. H. "Tangle of Ethics," *Harvard Business Review*, Vol. XXXVIII, January 1960, pp. 59-62.

There is a confusion surrounding the ethical problems in industry, which the author claims is due to that what seems to the businessman like an "impossible ideal" meeting head-on the "practical necessities" of his trade or commerce, and the inevitable compromise or betrayal of one or the other leaving him with a bad conscience.

Moley, R., "Business Morality," *Newsweek*, March 6, 1961.

Moore, Robert. "Business Philosophy," *Bulletin of the Business History Society*, Vol. XXIV, December 1950, pp. 196-206.

"The Moral History of U.S. Business," *Fortune*, Vol. 22, December 1949, p. 143.

General review of the American evolution of business ethics over the past 200 years. Article states that the American businessmen have always had moral compulsions which affect their business drive. Concludes by inferring that American Business has never long remained complacent about its moral motives and purposes which shows man's spirituality through divine discontent.

"Morals in the Market Place," *America*, Vol. 99, September 20, 1958, p. 639.

Newberg, W. C. "Challenge to Business Leadership," *Vital Speeches*, Vol. XXV, pp. 618-621.

Newman, L. H. "Human Values for Management Engineers," *Advanced Management*, Vol. XXIV, July 1959, pp. 15-17.

Concise article giving seven principles for managers to follow in order to promote good philosophies. It is emphasized that these principles are guides to action.

Nordling, Rolf. "Social Responsibilities of Today's Industrial Leader," *Advanced Management*, Vol. 22, April 1957, pp. 18-22.

A French industrialist examines the social responsibilities of industrial management and reaches a conclusion similar to American—the problem is to equate it with the economic goals of the enterprise.

Norris, Louis W. "Moral Hazards of the Executive," *Harvard Business Review*, September-October, 1961, pp. 73-79.

A discussion of problems faced by businessmen. Norris believes that 1) Compromise is necessary, but not because of expedience alone, 2) Integrity is the chief requirement of the executive, 3) Decisions are made without all the facts and must be considered in that light, 4) responsibility of decisions be with the top executive and, 5) that a man is big enough for a job if he is adequate to deal with the moral issues put before him.

Odegard, P. H. "Toward a Responsible Bureaucracy," *Annals of the American Academy of Political and Social Science*, Vol. CCLXLII, March 1954, pp. 18-29.

Ohmann, O. A. "Search for a Managerial Philosophy" *Harvard Business Review*, September-October, 1957, pp. 41-51.

Why a business is a social institution as well as a profit making enterprise. The reasons and the implications for the businessman's conduct.

————. "Skyhooks," *Harvard Business Review*, May 1955, pp. 33-41.

People have lost faith in the basic values of our economic society. "Man looks for new Skyhooks, for an abiding faith around which life's experience can be integrated and given meaning." Importance of what happens to people in the course of producing.

Oliver, Henry M. "Trends Toward a New Moral Philosophy for Business," *Business Horizons*, Vol. I, Spring, 1958.

Orton, W. A. "Business and Ethics," *Fortune*, October 1948, pp. 118-124.

Packard, David. "A Management Code of Ethics," *Supervisory Management*, Vol.3, June 1958, pp. 22-3.

Discussion of need for universal code of ethics and what tenets this code should be based upon. Concludes by relating that code must be based on high objectivity, "the preservation of liberty."

Patterson, W. A. "Growing Dimension of Management," *Commercial and Financial Chronicle*, Vol. CLXXXVIII, August 28, 1958.

Peak, George W. "The More 'Personal' Responsibilities of the Top Executive," *Advanced Management*, Vol. 22, No. 12, December 1957, pp. 13-14.

Discussion deals with additional more personal responsibilities of example setting, self-development, time utilization, and being mortal. Best example setting guide is "Do unto others as you know a top executive ought to do unto you if you were one of the others." Being mortal is being human, keeping in good health both mind and body.

Perry, G. "Responsibility of the Businessman," *Vital Speeches,* Vol. XXVI, May 15, 1960, pp. 458-461.

Pirenne, Henri. "The Stages in the Social History of Capitalism," *American Historical Review,* Vol. XIX, April 1914, pp. 494-515.

Pope, Liston. "Is There a Decline in U.S. Morals?" *U.S. News and World Report,* May 21, 1962, pp. 60-64.

A discussion on some basic changes in this society which might have led to current scandals. Bigness in everything seems to be one of the great changes. Governmental intervention seems to be another of these changes.

"A Positive Code of Ethics," *Business Week,* June 17, 1961, p. 166.

An affirmative code of conduct is offered such that every business manager must have an obligation to society that overrides any other obligation he may have.

Powlison, Keith. "The Profit Motive Compromised," *Harvard Business Review,* March 1950, pp. 102-108.

"Price Fixing: What's the Answer?" *Dun's Review,* May 1961, pp. 36-38.

There is no apparent answer, and executives wind up in the middle of a conflict caused by inadequate legislation possibly.

"The Public Looks at Business," *Harvard Business Review,* March 1949.

"Public Relations Today," *Business Week,* Vol. 1609, July 2, 1960, pp. 40-62.

A lengthy news report on the vice of the practice of public relations in American business, emphasizing the growing concentration on its job of helping to uplift ethical standards.

"Purchasing Ethics: Is There a Problem?" *Purchasing,* Vol. 45, September 1, 1958, pp. 55-7.

Discussion of Sales Management's article on salesmen's view on bribery of buyers and a defense of purchasing agents.

Randall, C. B. "Free Enterprise is Not a Hunting License," *Advanced Management,* June 1952, pp. 22-5.

The freedom that we enjoy in the free enterprise system is the last strength of civilized man. We must preserve it and develop it by understanding it and with scrupulous integrity maintaining it against socialism.

Reagan, Michael. "Seven Fallacies of Business in Politics," *Harvard Business Review,* March-April, 1960, pp. 60-68.

An attack on various reasons promulgated for entrance into politics by businessmen. The author believes that corporations should seek legislation through traditional techniques—interest groups—rather than elected offices.

Rice, John R. "Existentialism for the Businessman," *Harvard Business Review,* Vol. 38, March-April, 1960, pp. 135-43.

Discussion of how existentialism in the world penetrates the present day business decisions. Author points out that Judeo Christian philosophy and the philosophy of an individual's actions contributing to his own well begin is becoming acceptable in business today.

Robbins, W. David. "Is Competitive Pricing Legal?" *Harvard Business Review,* Vol. 35, No. 6, November-December, 1957, p. 83.

The Federal Trade Commission and the courts are sincerely interested in pricing, but sometimes it seems that the Robinson-Patman Act protects competitors, not competition.

Romney, George. "Danger: Citizenship By Proxy," *The Quarterly Review of Public Relations,* Vol. 5, Summer, 1960, pp. 2-5.

While arguing for the need to encourage more participation in public affairs by employees, this industrial leader believes the job should be done as a function of public relations programs, rather than have special staff put in charge, thus give the idea of coercion.

————. "Politics Is for People," *Readers Digest,* Vol. LXXVI, May 1960, pp. 241-244.

Schell, H. V. "Measuring the Efficiency of Management From a Society's Viewpoint," *Advanced Management,* Vol. 24, September 1959, pp. 4-7.

Today, management is well aware of the many available methods of measuring efficiency and of the large stakes involved. However, only a few firms have devised programs aimed at the development of a working atmosphere in which the desire of these employees for status and prestige is given full recognition and encouragement.

Schleh, E. C. "Unfolding Management Perspective," *Advanced Management,* Vol. XXV, May 1960, pp. 83-85.

Schnepp, G. J. "Survey of Opinion on the Industry Council Plan," *American Catholic Sociological Review,* June 1957, pp. 75-83.

Selekman, B. M. "Cynicism and Managerial Morality," *Harvard Business Review,* Vol. 36, September 1958, pp. 61-71.

Discussion of attitudes of cynics in business who assert that businessmen are basically selfish, self aggrandizing, and exploitative of their fellowman. Author feels that this is completely contrary to what thoughtful businessmen assume about nature when they emphasize social and ethical goals.

Sheely, J. E. "Reciprocity: Legal or Illegal?" *Oil Paint and Drug Reporter,* Vol. 179, February 27, 1961, p. 7.

Investigation into the legality of certain inter-company buying policies and procedures.

Shield, L. P. "Over-all, Long-range Direction of American Business," *Commercial and Financial Chronicle,* Vol. CLXXXVII, March 13, 1958.

Sinclair, J. S. "Role of Business in Public Affairs," *Management Record,* Vol. XXII, January 1960, pp. 6-10.

Slichter, Sumner H. "The Businessman in a Laboristic Economy," *Fortune,* September 1949, pp. 108-118.

————. "Better Than We Think," *Atlantic Monthly,* Vol. 185, January 1950, pp. 46-9.

Many individuals today regard the world as experiencing a moral crisis that is bound to leave the future of mankind very dark. The author rejects this hypothesis while citing the record that marks the current century as one of remarkable moral progress.

Sloane, L. "Reciprocity Doesn't Have to be a Dirty Word," *Purchasing,* Vol. 46, March 30, 1959, pp. 80-1.

Discussion of how, if used correctly, a policy of reciprocity is both legal and ethical.

Smith, J. S. "Challenges for Business Statesmen," *Public Relations Journal,* February 1958, pp. 15-18.

Smith, Richard Austin. "The Incredible Electrical Conspiracy, Part I," *Fortune,* Vol. 63, April, 1961, pp. 132-137, 170.

First part of a report on the electrical industry price-fixing case, stressing the back-room meetings which were used to reach agreement on market sharing.

————. "The Incredible Electrical Conspiracy, Part II," *Fortune,* Vol. 63, May 1961, pp. 161-164, 210.

Second part of the report on the electrical industry case, emphasizing the Justice Department's investigation and the legal procedures.

Snyder, John I. "The Impact of Automation," *Challenge,* Vol. 10, May 1962, pp. 20-23.

An interview with the head of automation equipment manufacturer reveals his backing of a shorter work week, emergency government measures, and labor-management coordination as means for solving problems brought by automation.

Stewart, R. N. "Ethical Principles in Today's Business," *Office Executive,* Vol. 35, No. 6, 1960, pp. 13-16.

A discussion of the problems encountered in older codes and a presentation and discussion of the author's four-point code of ethics.

Stryker, P. "The Pirates of Management," *Fortune,* June 1961.

Many cases of pirating are discussed. The author justifies pirating on the grounds that it brings good managers to jobs when they are needed.

Sullivan, A. M. "Business Ethics: Policy or Principle," *Dun's Review,* Vol. 74, November 1959, p. 67.

Sullivan debates whether ethics are absolute and unchanging or relative and varying. He does not settle the question.

Summer, C. E. "Managerial Mind," *Harvard Business Review,* Vol. 37, January-February, 1959, pp. 69-78.

The author raises the interesting question of whether the thinking of business executives is characterized by well defined qualities and attitudes as is the thinking of professional scientists.

"Survey of Business Opinions and Experience by Corporate Directors and Business Officers," *The Conference Board Business Record,* September 1961, pp. 31-34.

This concise article places the responsibility for ethical practices on boards of directors.

Taylor, H. P. "Business Responsibility in a Changing World," *Credit and Financial Management,* Vol. LII, February 1950, pp. 26-27.

Tead, Ordway. "Business Leadership in the Decade Ahead," *Advanced Management,* February 1955, pp. 5-9.

Tead suggests that business must recognize the needs of the whole man. He sees the future as one in which man will have a new grasp of the nature of man and a new awareness of the interdependence of business, the total economy and of our democracy.

————. "Ethical Challenge to Modern Administration," *Advanced Management,* Vol. XXV, October 1960, pp. 8-12.

Teadway, L. "Payola in the Purchasing Department," *Purchasing,* Vol. 48, March 28, 1960, pp. 86-8.
Investigation of policies of some large corporations in using their purchasing power to increase their sales power.

Theobald, Robert. "Needed: A New Dimension To Collective Bargaining," *Challenge,* Vol. 10, April 1962, pp. 27-31.
A call for government to play a larger role in collective bargaining in an effort to find ways to use both labor and machinery surpluses for benefit of this country and the world.

Thimm, A. L. "Ideological Pitfalls in Contemporary Management Practices," *Advanced Management,* Vol. XXV, August 1960, pp. 13-15.

Thomas, Norman, "The Double Standard of Ethics," *The Humanist,* Vol. 18, September 1958, pp. 266-273.
This article was aptly published in *The Humanist.* Thomas convincingly states that man is all important, and ethically he should not do as a member of the group that which he would not do as an individual.

Thomson, D. J. "Responsibilities of a Corporate Enterprise in the Community, State and Nation," *Advanced Management,* Vol. XXV, February 1960, pp. 14-16.

"Today's Civic-Minded Executives," *Management Review,* Vol. 46, February 1957, pp. 28-29.
While civic-minded executives still write checks to charitable organizations, many businessmen are not content to discharge their public responsibility with money alone. Instead, more and more executives are donating of their time and talent to various civic projects.

Toynbee, A. J. "Thinking Ahead: Will Businessmen Be Civic Servants?" *Harvard Business Review,* Vol. XXXVI, September 1958, p. 23.
A rather lengthy story projecting thought about the future 50 years from now. An excess of time is spent incomparison with the Greco-Roman civilization.

"Transformation of American Capitalism," *Fortune,* Vol. XLIII, February 1951, pp. 78-83.

Urwick, L. F. "Purpose of a Business," *Dun's Review and Modern Industry,* Vol. LXVI, November 1955, p. 51.
Author feels that the basic purpose of business is social service both in policy and in actual deed. He makes extensive use of quotations from other well known authors.

"U.S.A., The Permanent Revolution," *Fortune,* February 1951.

Van Buskirk, A. B. "Responsibilities of American Business Leaders," *Vital Speeches,* Vol. XXV, September 1, 1959, pp. 690-693.

"Verdict on Labor by Top Management," *Dun's Review and Modern Industry,* Vol. 74, February 1960, pp. 65-66.
A report of survey of top management people which reveals that, despite their differences, the business leaders as a whole see labor as a constructive force, but believe they may be starting to go too far.

Viteles, M. S. "Human Relations and the Humanities in the Education of Business Leaders," *Personnel Psychology,* Vol. XII, Spring, 1959, pp. 1-28.
Viteles proposes an enlargement of knowledge and understanding to the worker. He suggests the use of employee-attitude surveys to evaluate the interests, attitudes, and values of the employees, and to use the findings for the benefit of the company-employee relationship.

Walton, Clarence C. "Ethical Theory, Society Expectations and Marketing Practices," *Social Responsibilities of Marketing,* William Stevens, Editor. Proceedings of the Winter conference, American Marketing Association, pp. 7-25.
An analysis on the considerations in the marketing area of business with respect to ethical problems. Some justification on these practices.

Watkins, R. J. "Business Ethics and World Conflict," *Dun's Review,* Vol. LIX, September 1951, pp. 15-17.

Weisskipf, W., and Thain, R. "Value Research in Business, Economics Long Overdue," *Business and Society,* Vol. I, Autumn, 1960, pp. 3-9.

Wheeler, W. H., Jr. "Industry's New Responsibility," *Management Review,* Vol. XXXVIII, December 1949, pp. 646-651.

————. "Management for Freedom," *Management Review,* Vol. XLIII, February 1954, pp. 74-75.
A foreshadowing of the executive swing in thinking to include the public interest.

White, R. N. "Consultants' Concept of the Meaning of Modern Management," *Office Executive,* Vol. XXXIV, September 1959, p. 56.
A good outline of the functional areas of management and the elements of managing. Charts are included.

Willard, W. R. "A Management Challenge," *Advanced Management,* Vol. 24, February 1959, pp. 9-10.
The author presents a challenge to management to do something about individualism. He is referring to the problem of the submergence of the individual and the loss of individuality in our present day corporate society.

Wilson, Robert E. "Answering Critics of Business Ethics," *Credit and Financial Management,* Vol. LVII, July 1955, pp. 18-19.
Brief article listing six factors which have been responsible for a steady improvement in business ethics: depression, public sentiment, fair business dealing, honor of the leader, employee morale, ideology of the churches and college.

————. "Ethics in Modern Business," *The Commercial and Financial Chronicle,* Vol. 188, August 28, 1958, pp. 15-29.
An appraisal of business ethics—concluding they are higher than ever, but stating disappointment in business' failure to fight against corruption in city, state and national government.

Wooten, Paul. "What Makes A Fair Labor Law?" *Dun's Review and Modern Industry,* Vol. 72, September 1958, pp. 145-146.
Presentation of the ten key provisions that the Eisenhower administration was supporting as the basis for fair labor legislation.

"World and the Spirit," *Business Week,* Vol. 26, November 14, 1959, p. 176.
Attempt to explain a new approach which will shift ethics to a more spiritual plane by having business accept the ethics of religion which

specifically involve Judeo-Christian morality. Criticism of big business which appears to keep a clear distinction between religion and economics.

Worthy, J. "Religion and Its Role in the World of Business," *Journal of Business,* Vol. XXX, October 1958, pp 203-303.

Worthy advocates a return to ethical principles expressed in religious faith rather than in the present secular trend. He places the blame for the void of religious faith in business practice on the theologians and preachers.

ADDRESSES

Bartels, Robert. "Business Ethics—Compliance or Conviction"

An address given for The University of Southern California, Los Angeles, California, May 4, 1961.

A review of ethics in business, tracing the early effort in this direction and moving forward to the recent electrical price fixing conspiracy.

A definition of business ethics, relating it to the social and religious areas, and looking forward to the apparent improvement that has been made.

Estes, Bay E. Jr. "Industrial Research."

An address delivered before the Industrial Designers Institute, Chicago, February 1962, p. 13.

"In our country, cult of growth for growth's sake parading as progress but looking very much like the statism that other lands have accepted, is loudly proclaiming its supposed superiority over our traditions of individual dignity and liberty."

"We speak of 'the economy' as if it were a machine and we chart its 'growth' in dollars of 'gross national product', which are as fictional in meaning as they are diluted in real value by inflation. We ignore the reality that the economy is not products—it is people—and economics is not statistics but rather the material manifestations of human action and the satisfactions of underlying freedom of choice."

McElroy, Neil. "Responsibility of Business in Public Affairs."

An address at the 1961 United Fund Campaign National Leaders Conference, Dayton, June 6, 1961.

A positive statement in favor of voluntary assumption by business of responsibility in civic affairs to maintain a sound balance between government and what people do for themselves.

Miller, J. Irwin. "The Theological Basis for Social Action," New York: National Council of Churches of Christ in the U.S.A., 1958.

An address delivered at the 1958 Convention of Christian Churches (Disciples of Christ), St. Louis, Missouri.

Mr. Miller refers to passages from history and the Bible that support his belief that men do not need to be *told* what they ought to do, but rather that they be reminded—that they really knew all the time what the proper course was, but had, over the years, chosen to ignore it.

—————. "The World of Business and the Church," New York: National Council of Churches of Christ in the U.S.A., 1961.

An address delivered before the National Council of Church's General Board as the opening function of a campaign for a new Interchurch Center in Chicago.

Mr. Miller speaks on the subjects of "Business and Power"; how to be "business-like"; business has a boss; absorbing cost increases; and finally a summing up with "the place of the church."

Parker, Jack S. "The New Dynamics of Corporate Relations Work."

An address at the National Association of Manufacturers Industrial Relations Institute, Miami, April 5, 1961.

A description of General Electric's reorganized relationships program which coordinates all affairs for dealing with claimant publics through a centralized operation.

Rockefeller, David. "Responsibilities of Business in a Troubled World."

An address before the Wharton School Alumni Society, Philadelphia, November 16, 1961.

An enlarged role of leadership in both domestic and world affairs is seen as business' main responsibility today along with effective production and distribution of the sorts of goods and services customers want.

CASES

Standard Oil Company of New Jersey v. United States, in report of Attorney-General's National Committee to Study Anti-Trust Laws, 1955, pp. 5-8.

Basis to Sherman Act construction was the "Rule of Reason." Outline of its limitations, scope and main line of future development was made. Clarified relationship between the act and the common law. A new look at a much known controversy.

United States v. Aluminum Co. of America. 148 F 2d 416.

Alcoa was accused of having a monopoly of interstate and foreign commerce of manufacture and sale of "virgin" aluminum ingot, and that it be dissolved and further that the company and defendant, Aluminum Limited (Canada) had entered into a conspiracy in restraint of commerce. The lower court dismissed the complaint but the upper court reversed this decision and cause remanded further proceedings.

United States v. Pullman, 50 F. supp. 123.

United States charged company with monopoly dealings, price fixing. U.S. asked for separation of operating and manufacturing divisions, and free choice of pullman cars to all buyers. Also removal of exclusive deals. U.S. won the case.

UNPUBLISHED

Box, Jay Richard. "A Survey of Management Codes of Ethics in the Metal Products Industry." Unpublished Dissertation, The Ohio State University, Columbus, 1958.

In this study, the author recounts the history of ethics, surveys the metal industries, and finds little use of formal ethical codes. There is evidence of only a few instances where punishment was netted out for violations of ethics. He gives several suggestions for better ethics and also lists an excellent bibliography.

Eby, Barnett Sanford. "Economics and the Concept of Justice." Princeton, New Jersey: Unpublished Doctoral Dissertation, Princeton University, 1951.